Cognitive Development

Cognitive Development provides a detailed and accessible account of three main areas: theories of cognitive development, the development of measured intelligence and the development of moral understanding. The theories of Piaget, Vygotsky and Bruner and the information processing approach are also introduced. The book is suitable for the AQA-A A2 level examination and students studying cognitive development for the first time at undergraduate level.

Lisa Oakley is a Senior Lecturer in Psychology at Manchester Metropolitan University.

Routledge Modular Psychology

Series editors: Cara Flanagan is a Reviser for AS and A2 level Psychology and an experienced teacher and examiner. Philip Banyard is Associate Senior Lecturer in Psychology at Nottingham Trent University and a Chief Examiner for AS and A2 level Psychology.

The *Routledge Modular Psychology* series is a completely new approach to introductory-level psychology, tailor-made to the new modular style of teaching. Each short book covers a topic in more detail than any large textbook can, allowing teacher and student to select material exactly to suit any particular course or project.

The books have been written especially for those students new to higher-level study, whether at school, college or university. They include specially designed features to help with technique, such as a model essay at an average level with an examiner's comments to show how extra marks can be gained. The authors are all examiners and teachers at the introductory level.

The *Routledge Modular Psychology* texts are all user-friendly and accessible and use the following features:

- practice essays with specialist commentary to show how to achieve a higher grade
- chapter summaries to assist with revision
- progress and review exercises
- glossary of key terms
- summaries of key research
- further reading to stimulate ongoing study and research
- cross-referencing to other books in the series

For more details on our AS, A2 and *Routledge Modular Psychology* publications visit our website at www.a-levelpsychology.co.uk

Also available in this series (titles listed by syllabus section):

Cognitive Development

Lisa Oakley

Routledge
Taylor & Francis Group

LONDON AND NEW YORK

First published 2004
by Routledge
27 Church Road, Hove, East Sussex BN3 2FA

Simultaneously published in the USA and Canada
by Routledge
270 Madison Avenue, New York NY 10016

Routledge is an imprint of the Taylor & Francis Group

Typeset in Times and Frutiger by Keystroke,
Jacaranda Lodge, Wolverhampton
Printed and bound in Great Britain by
TJ International Ltd, Padstow, Cornwall
Paperback cover design by Anú Design

This publication has been produced with paper manufactured to strict
environmental standards and with pulp derived from sustainable forests.

British Library Cataloguing in Publication Data
A catalogue record for this book is available from the British Library

Library of Congress Cataloging-in-Publication Data
Oakley, Lisa.
  Cognitive development / Lisa Oakley.
    p.   cm. – (Routledge modular psychology series)
Includes bibliographical references and index.
    ISBN 0-415-24234-7 (hbk.) – ISBN 0-415-24235-5 (pbk.)
    1. Cognition–Textbooks. 2. Developmental
psychology–Textbooks. I. Title. II. Routledge modular
psychology.

  BF311.O12 2004
  155.4′13–dc22   2003022844

ISBN 0-415-24234-7 (hbk)
ISBN 0-415-24235-5 (pbk)

To my parents – John and Margaret Denning

Contents

Illustrations

Figures

Tables

Acknowledgements

I would like to thank Cara Flanagan for her help and advice throughout the writing of this book. I would also like to thank Dr Nick Lund who has also helped and advised during the writing process. Finally I would like to thank my family for supporting me in this.

1

Introduction

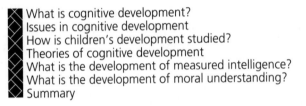

What is cognitive development?
Issues in cognitive development
How is children's development studied?
Theories of cognitive development
What is the development of measured intelligence?
What is the development of moral understanding?
Summary

The topic of this book is *Cognitive Development* which is a major area of study within **developmental psychology.** Developmental psychology is defined by Birch (1998) as 'the study of the psychological changes that take place between birth and old age' (p. 1). The aim of developmental psychology is to explain and describe the changes that occur from birth through to adulthood.

However, during childhood there is the greatest amount of change and the most dramatic development. Therefore the developments that occur during the period of birth to adolescence are commonly the focus of developmental psychology. Developmental psychology includes the study of all aspects of children's psychological development. This includes physical, social, language, and emotional, intellectual and cognitive development. This book focuses upon cognitive development.

However, it should be noted that there is an increasing amount of research into adulthood, and research including adulthood is becoming known as **life span development**.

What is cognitive development?

The word cognitive originally comes from a Latin word *cognoscere*, which means *to know*. Therefore cognitive activities include all the psychological processes and activities involved in thinking and knowing. These include how information is acquired, processed and organised. **Cognitive development** is the study of how these processes develop in children and young people, and how they become more efficient and effective in their understanding of the world and in their mental processes. Children's thinking is not the same as adult thinking. As a child develops, their thinking changes, and cognitive development is the study of these changes and developments.

Cognitive psychology includes the study of memory and perception. Cognitive development includes the study of a number of areas but those covered within this book will be:

- Theories of cognitive development. The theories of Piaget and Vygotsky will be discussed and reference will also be made to the information processing approaches. These theories have been applied to education and the ways in which they have been applied will be discussed
- The development of measured intelligence. Of central importance to this area is the debate around nature and nurture (see later). Issues of genetics, environmental and cultural factors will be considered.
- The development of moral understanding. The theories of Kohlberg and Piaget will inform the discussion of the development of moral understanding. It is also important to consider Eisenberg's theory of pro-social reasoning as this offers an alternative explanation of children's moral development. The influence of gender and culture on this area of cognitive development is also an important factor to consider.

Issues in cognitive development

There are three key issues which relate to the study of cognitive development.

Nature versus nurture

Nature refers to inherited factors, especially genes, and includes events that occur as the child naturally matures, e.g. puberty. **Nurture** refers to the environment the child develops in and this includes the experiences that each child has throughout their development. The fundamental question concerns what influences development, nature or nurture – but more than this, how much does each influence and how does this influence occur? The nature/nurture debate is especially important in the discussion of the development of measured intelligence.

This debate is central to many other issues considered within developmental psychology such as physical abilities, personality and gender differences. It is likely that if you are studying other aspects of developmental psychology you will encounter this question again. It is a controversial issue as it is often difficult to separate the influence of nature and nurture and draw any definite conclusions (Birch, 1998).

Experience versus maturation

Just as it is difficult to separate the influence of genetics and the environment, it is also difficult to establish how much of cognitive development is dependent on biological maturation, which is genetically programmed, and how much is dependent on experience. Some psychologists suggest that maturation is the key factor. Cognitive development occurs as the child matures and this development is pre-programmed into the genes. This idea means that children can only develop when they are biologically ready and that there is little point in trying to encourage development until the child is ready. However the alternative idea is that children develop through experience and practice, and the more they practise the better and more efficient they become. Again it is difficult to solve this debate, but current thinking is that it is probably a combination of these two factors that is the best explanation of cognitive development (Birch, 1998).

Competence and performance

A final issue, which will be important when reviewing the empirical evidence in this book, is the difference between competence and performance. There is a difference between what children are actually able to do and understand, and how they use their knowledge and ability. Therefore children often perform below their actual level of ability when being tested. Many parents will tell you of the times when their children had developmental checks. During these checks children fail to do tasks which they do with little effort at home. For example an 18 month old may regularly stack many bricks at home but fails to achieve stacking three at the developmental check. Why is this? They may underperform for a variety of reasons. These include worrying about the tests, not concentrating, not understanding what they have to do, being wary of the stranger testing them and being in an unfamiliar environment. Obviously when decisions about how children develop cognitively are made on the basis of tests, the reasons for underperformance are very important. It is an issue which is especially relevant to the work of Piaget, as will be seen in Chapter 2 (Birch, 1998).

How is children's development studied?

There are a variety of methods used to study children's development. These include

Naturalistic observation

Children are studied in their natural environment and often they are unaware that they are being studied. Their behaviour is not usually restricted or interfered with. This method has allowed psychologists to learn about the natural behaviour and development of children, and is less intrusive for children than other methods. Piaget used this method and the clinical interview (see below) when developing his theory of cognitive development. (See Chapter 2 for Piaget's theory.) However, often parents may know that their children are being watched, and this may affect the way they behave and in turn their children's behaviour, so the behaviour observed may not be natural. Children themselves may realise they are being watched. Also the observer has to make records and judgements about the child's behaviour and this is obviously open to bias. In addition if the researcher does not interfere in any way they may not obtain the information which they require, as the child may not exhibit the behaviour they want to study. This can be a very time-consuming method, which may not always yield the required information.

Controlled observation

The disadvantages of naturalistic observation can be overcome to some extent by controlled observation. In this technique there are strict guidelines as to what to observe, how to observe and when to observe. The researcher may manipulate or control a situation to investigate behaviour they want to study. This allows observation of basically natural behaviour, but the results are more reliable and easier to compare with observations of other children, and variables are more controlled than in naturalistic observation. Disadvantages are that behaviour is not completely natural, and that the setting may be unusual and therefore have an influence on the behaviour observed. Also the researcher may fail to note very important behaviour because it falls outside the factors they are observing.

Cross-sectional studies

This method allows researchers to compare different age groups of children with each other at the same point in time. For example researchers may take a sample of 4-, 5-, 6-, 7- and 8-year-old children in the same school at the same time. If they wanted to discover how children's moral understanding develops, they could compare groups of children who are different ages and see how they differ in the ways in which they deal with moral problems. The advantage to this method is that it can provide detailed information about development in a short amount of time; researchers don't need to wait until the children develop to continue the research. It is a relatively cheap method of investigation. It is also easy to replicate. It can identify differences between age groups and is therefore useful for studying age-related changes and group differences.

However, researchers are comparing children who may not be comparable. They may be different in individual characteristics and there is also evidence that different cohorts of children experience different environments and therefore may not be comparable. This is known as the **cohort effect**. Also, this approach does not allow us to study individual development and investigate individual children. (For examples of this method see Rest, 1983b:103.)

Longitudinal studies

One of the disadvantages of the cross-sectional study is that it may not be valid to make comparisons between different children, for the reasons discussed above. Longitudinal studies overcome this problem by studying the same children over a period of time, testing at regular intervals. In the example above, children's development of moral understanding would be investigated by asking each of the same children their solutions to moral problems when that child is aged 4, 5, 6 and so on. This is a repeated measures design and therefore the variables discussed above are controlled. As the same children are being used, differences will not be due to individual differences between different children. This method allows researchers to identify factors that may influence development and to study individual development. Finally it allows researchers to investigate whether behaviour is stable over time.

The disadvantage to this approach is that it is very time consuming and expensive. Results take a long time to collect and publish, and therefore new information may take many years to discover. Results may seem dated when published, as current research questions may not be addressed. Also there is a high dropout rate as participants may choose not to continue with the research and may lose interest (this is known as **attrition**). This may affect the reliability of the results, as the sample who choose to remain may be biased in some way (e.g. they are the keen ones or ones with 'better' lives). It may be that the parents of the children that remain in the sample support them and encourage them to continue with the research. It may be just as interesting and important to the researchers to obtain the information from children who do not remain in the sample. (For examples of this method see Sameroff et al., 1987:71; Eisenberg et al., 1987; Eisenberg & Fabes, 1991:109.)

Twin and family studies

One method used to investigate the difference between nature and nurture (see above) is to compare twins. Identical twins known as monozygotic twins share the same genetic makeup – they have 100% the same genes. Therefore any differences in their development cannot be due to a difference in their inherited characteristics (nature) but must be due to their nurture. This allows psychologists to study different aspects of development and try to establish whether nature or nurture is most influential in specific areas of development.

However, it is not as simple as it first seems to study identical twins and draw conclusions about their development and the effect of nurture. Twins who are brought up together share not only their genetic makeup but also their environment, therefore it is difficult to separate the influence of the two factors. Equally, identical twins are not always treated the same so we cannot estimate how much 'nurture' they shared. This is a difficult topic to investigate and the study of twins has aided our understanding, but there are problems with the use of twin studies – for a more detailed discussion of this topic see Chapter 4 entitled The Development of Measured Intelligence. (For examples of this method see Bouchard & McGue, 1981; Pederson et al., 1992:64.)

Interviews

During interviews, questions may be asked of a child or their parents and carers to discover information about particular aspects of development. Piaget used the **clinical interview** when developing his theory of cognitive development. This is called the clinical technique because it is similar to the technique a doctor uses when consulting with a patient, involving fairly open questions. Interviews can provide information that observation cannot provide. For example, through observation you would be unlikely to know what reasons children have for the moral choices they make, but through interviews you would be able to ask. Social desirability may be an issue for interviews. Individuals may say what they think the researcher wants them to or what is socially acceptable. For example, it is unlikely that many parents will tell an interviewer that they are racist and they allow their child to express racist views, as this is not seen as acceptable. However, they may indeed support these views privately. There are sometimes problems with standardisation of interviews, as different interviewees may introduce bias; this can occur either when the interview is being conducted or when the results are being analysed. As interviews rely on language and young children's language is limited, this factor may make interviews unsuitable until a certain age, or indeed interviewers may misunderstand the responses given by children, therefore limiting the effectiveness of this method for use in developmental psychology. (For examples of this method see Piaget, 1932:84; Kohlberg, 1963: 99–100.)

Experiments

The use of experiments makes for reliable and valid research and results. Experiments are designed to control variables and to be easily replicable. Experiments allow for an investigation of cause and effect, and can lead to some firm conclusions. However, experiments are often limited, as a time limit is set for their completion. It is difficult to establish whether behaviour is consistent over time because often it is only tested once and thus provides a snapshot view, which may not be typical. Often experimental conditions are unnatural, restrictive and outside the experience of many children, and so results could be obtained which may not be a representation of the child's natural behaviour. This is obviously important if decisions about development are made on the basis of these findings.

Theories of cognitive development

There are a number of theories which have been developed to explain how cognitive development occurs in children. These theories attempt to describe how children's cognitive development occurs, what changes there are in thinking when they occur and what factors influence children's cognitive development. The discussion of theories in this book will include a description of those developed by Piaget and Vygotsky.

Jean Piaget was probably one of the most influential psychologists of the twentieth century. Piaget was the first to note that children's thinking was different from adult thinking and that at different ages children's thinking was different. He developed a stage theory of cognitive development based on his research. Piaget's theories had strong educational applications and had a profound influence on education and thinking about children. A discussion of his theory and its implications can be found in Chapter 2.

Vygotsky also saw children as active in their development. However, he differed in his approach and thinking from Piaget, and in some fundamental ways. Vygotsky's theory also has educational implications and a discussion of these, the theory and an evaluation can be found in Chapter 3.

What is the development of measured intelligence?

The question 'what is intelligence?' is one of the most controversial ones asked. There are wide disagreements about what intelligence actually is. Indeed psychologists cannot agree about whether there is in fact such a thing as one intelligence or whether it is made up of a number of different intelligences. Psychologists have developed tests which assess some but not all of the different areas of intelligence. These aspects can be measured and the term 'measured intelligence' describes these factors. The question is, how does this measured intelligence develop and what factors influence it? The key factors under discussion are nature (genetics etc.) and nurture (environmental and cultural factors). A discussion of the development of measured intelligence can be found in Chapter 4.

What is the development of moral understanding?

Morals are decisions or rules about what is right and what is wrong. Children do not appear to be born with these rules and the understanding of what is morally right and wrong. The development of moral understanding includes not only how children think about such issues but also how they behave in moral situations and how they feel about them.

Piaget developed a stage theory of moral development which, like his theory of cognitive development, sought to describe how children's moral understanding changes and develops. Kohlberg also developed a theory of moral development but his theory did not firmly attach ages to stages, and it extended into adulthood. However, the above theories have been challenged by Eisenberg, who suggested that pro-social reasoning is an essential part of moral development and one that Piaget and Kohlberg overlooked. She too developed a stage theory of moral reasoning. However, others such as Gilligan see gender as an important factor in moral development. Cultural differences are also seen to be influential in the development of moral understanding. A discussion of the development of moral reasoning can be found in Chapter 5.

Summary

Developmental psychologists study all aspects of development but tend to focus on the period from birth to adolescence. The study of cognitive development in children is part of the general study of developmental psychology. Cognitive development is the study of the changes and developments that occur in the thinking and reasoning in the child. There are many different methods which have been used to study children's development – naturalistic observation, controlled observation, longitudinal studies, cross-sectional studies, experiments, interviews and twin studies. These methods all have advantages and disadvantages.

There are many different theories of cognitive development. Piaget and Vygotsky developed theories that sought to explain children's cognitive development and the factors that influence this development. Both theories had educational implications.

Another aspect of the cognitive development is the development of measured intelligence. Although psychologists cannot agree on a general definition of intelligence, aspects of intelligence can be measured. The main debate concerns what factors influence the development of this measured intelligence – specifically whether nature or nurture is more important.

The final aspect of cognitive development to be considered by this book is the development of moral understanding. Children develop their understanding and this seems to occur alongside general cognitive development. Piaget and Kohlberg developed theories to explain the changes that occur in children, and adult moral understanding. These theories were challenged by Eisenberg's stage model of pro-social reasoning. Other factors such as culture and gender are seen as influential.

1. Briefly define the following:
   Cognitive development.
   The development of moral understanding.
2. What are the advantages and disadvantages of naturalistic observation?
3. Briefly summarise what the nature–nurture debate is about.

Further reading

Lee, V. & Das Gupta, P. (Eds.) (1995) *Children's Cognitive and Language Development*, Blackwell – this book contains a detailed discussion of both cognitive and language development. There is a great deal of detail about influences on modern studies of cognitive development and a description of the major theories.

2

Piaget's theory of cognitive development

Introduction

The study of cognitive development is dominated by the theories of two key psychologists – Piaget and Vygotsky. Other theories have been developed but they usually have foundations based upon these key theories.

Jean Piaget (1896–1980) was one of the most influential theorists in the field of cognitive development. Piaget was a philosopher, biologist, educationalist and psychologist. He made the decision to study scientifically the way in which children develop knowledge.

It was Piaget who first noted that children were not just miniature replicas of adults, but in fact were different in the ways in which they thought about and interpreted the world. Piaget's idea was that adults did not simply know *more* than children, but that their knowledge was structured differently. Indeed, Piaget suggested that children at different stages of their development thought about and interpreted their worlds in different ways (Hummel, 1998). Piaget developed the idea of children as '"little scientists" who were engaged in active exploration, seeking understanding and knowledge' (Bee, 2000:164).

Principles of Piaget's theory

Piaget's theory of cognitive development was based on three main principles – those of assimilation, accommodation and equilibration. These will be explained below, however, first it is important to define the term 'schema'.

Schema is a cognitive representation of activities or things. When a baby is born it will have an innate schema for sucking in order to ensure that it can feed and therefore grow. As the baby grows this schema will become integrated with other feeding schemas as the baby's experience and nutrition changes.

Assimilation is the process of putting a new experience into already existing mental structure (schemas) (Hummel, 1998). Children develop cognitive structures to help them make sense of their world and when they encounter a new experience they place this into the schemas they have already developed. The process of assimilation is an active one. Children are not merely absorbing knowledge via a process of osmosis, they are actively engaged in the assimilation process. They are active insofar as they are selective – they do not absorb all the information they encounter.

Accommodation is the revising of an existing schema due to a new experience. For example, a child may have a schema that describes all flying objects as birds, but when he encounters a frisbee this does not fit the schema. It isn't alive; therefore a new schema is necessary.

As children develop they will encounter experiences which their existing schemas are incapable of explaining. Therefore they must develop new schemas in response to new experiences.

Equilibration is the process of seeking to achieve cognitive stability through assimilation and accommodation (Hummel, 1998). The child is constantly trying to interpret and understand the world while encountering new experiences. The child builds an understanding of the world and how it works, but this is constantly challenged by new experiences that conflict with their current understanding. They seek to develop schemas to help this interpretation process. The drive for equilibrium is that all these interpretations and schemas fit together and make a general picture of the world that is logical. However, equilibrium is a constantly changing thing, as each time a child encounters a new experience they are in a place of disequilibrium until assimilation or accommodation has taken place.

If we return to the example of the frisbee, when the child first encounters it they are in a state of confusion (i.e. not equilibrium) – 'It isn't alive, I can't explain it with my present schemas or ways of thinking'. Through accommodation and the development of new schemas the child returns to a state of equilibrium, until the next new experience.

Piaget's stage model of cognitive development

Piaget suggested that the child's cognitive development could be divided into stages. As the child develops and goes through the process of assimilation and accommodation, their brain will develop through the natural process of maturation, and therefore their understanding of the world matures and their ability to accurately interpret and predict the world develops. Piaget thought that there were clear links between children's cognitive development and the natural biological maturation of the brain. According to Piaget, cognitive development is an inevitable process – as the brain matures the thinking matures, and the understanding increases.

However, Piaget also saw interaction with the environment as an important factor in cognitive development. Biological maturation takes place over a period of time. Piaget thought that children's cognitive development was based to a large extent on their biological development. Piaget thought that cognitive development took place in stages, each new stage becoming possible as the brain matures.

Piaget developed a stage theory, based upon his research with children. This theory described different stages of cognitive development. Piaget's theory can be thought of as based upon the idea of a staircase. Each stage represents a step and each step represents more development and a higher level of cognitive ability. It is important to note that these stages are fixed in sequence. That is, you cannot complete the stages in any order other than that described in Figure 2.1.

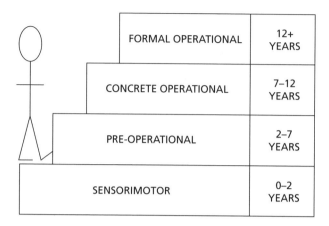

Figure 2.1 **Piaget's stage model of cognitive development**

The sensorimotor stage (0–2 years)

This stage encompasses the child from age 0–2 years. This is a stage of rapid development. During this stage the child will change from a fairly helpless newborn baby to a walking, talking toddler. This stage is dominated by sensory and motor activity. The newborn baby is dependent upon built-in schemas and reflexes, and is unable to imitate or integrate information. An example of a reflex is the sucking reflex, which is necessary for feeding and growing. As the child develops, their sensory and motor activities develop and increase, so that by the end of this stage they are able to imitate and integrate information to some degree. A 2-year-old child is capable of using objects to represent other objects, for example a cup can become a boat in a game. A more detailed description of this stage is presented in Table 2.1.

Object permanence is a key factor in this stage of Piaget's model. Piaget hypothesised that at 8 months the child develops the concept of object permanence, which is the knowledge that an object is 'permanently present, even if temporarily out of sight' (Smith, Cowie & Blades, 1998:40). Before a child acquires object permanence they will cease to look for an object when it is out of their field of vision – 'If I can't see it, it does not exist' – but once object permanence is acquired they will actively search for the object, as they know it still

Table 2.1 The six stages of the sensorimotor period according to Piaget

Stage	Approx. age (months)	Description
Reflexes	0–1m	Built in schemas and reflexes. No ability to imitate or integrate information. *Example* sucking reflex.
Primary circular reactions	1–4m	Phase composed of two elements. *Primary reactions* – reflexes / motor responses. *Circular reactions* – described as circular as they are repeated. Focus on infant's own body. No distinction between self and outside world. *Example* repeatedly shaking a rattle.
Secondary circular reactions	4–10m	Focus changes from own body to objects. Infant begins to develop small amount of control over surroundings. *Example* learns to kick at an activity gym to make it move. There is a degree of intention. Concept **Object Permanence** acquired at 8 months.
Co-ordination of secondary circular reactions	10–12m	Characterised by combining schemas to solve problems / achieve goals. *Example* use kicking schema to kick toys out of the way to get to pet cat.
Tertiary circular reactions	12–18m	Trial and error methods to learn about objects. Increase in mobility allows development of exploration

continued . . .

Table 2.1 continued		
Stage	**Approx. age (months)**	**Description**
		and experimentation. Learns to solve problems and about environment. *Example* tastes dirt in the garden, not everything tastes nice.
Internal representation	18–24m	Learns that objects and individuals can be represented by symbols. Previous behaviour can be imitated. Referred imitation. Solutions to problems become more complex, beginning of mental action. *Example* use cup as a boat whilst playing.

exists, so it must be somewhere. Object permanence is important because it demonstrates that the child has mentally represented the object.

The pre-operational stage (2–6 years)

This stage is divided into two sub-stages. These are the preconceptual period and the intuitive period. These two sub-stages are described below.

The preconceptual period (2–4 years)

This stage is characterised by an increase in language development, continuation of symbolic / internal representation and the development of imaginative play. The child begins to use symbols and language to represent things.

Limitations on thinking are due to **egocentrism** and **animism**. The term egocentrism is used as the child can only view the world from their perspective and finds it difficult to understand any other perspective. Animism is the tendency to attribute feelings and intentions to inanimate objects, e.g. Teddy feels sad.

Piaget investigated egocentrism in children by the use of the Three Mountains Test.

Piaget developed the Three Mountains Test to investigate egocentrism. A child is shown a 3D scene with mountains that differ in size and colour. Then the child picks from a set of drawings or models. First they choose the picture or models that represent how *they* see the scene, i.e. their view or perspective. Then they are asked to pick out a drawing that shows how *someone else* at a different angle sees the scene. Gzesh and Surber (1985) found that children usually choose the picture depicting their own viewpoint again (Bee, 2000). Piaget thought this failure was due to egocentrism. The child has not yet cognitively developed the ability to view the world from another perspective.

The intuitive period (4–6 years)

This stage is characterised by the development of mental ordering and classification. It is intuitive because the child has no idea about concepts/principles that underlie the classification.

Conservation is the realisation that quantity or amount does not change when nothing has been added or taken away from an object or collection of objects, despite changes in form or spatial arrangements (Pulaski, 1980). The ability to conserve is an important aspect of a child's cognitive development. Conservation experiments are a key part of Piaget's theory. Piaget considered children at this stage to be unable to conserve. He tested conservation of: liquid, volume, mass, number, length, weight and area. This chapter will now detail two examples of these experiments.

Piaget tested children's ability to conserve liquid by presenting them with two glasses of liquid.

Question
Which glass contains the most liquid?
Answer
Both the same.

Then the liquid is poured into two glasses of different sizes.

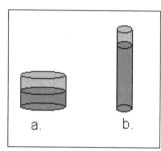

Question
Which glass contains the most liquid?
Answer
(Before the ability to conserve) **Glass b** because it's higher.
(When able to conserve) **They are both the same**, one is long and thin the other is short and fat.

Before the child is able to conserve they judge by appearance that glass b has more, as the level is higher. After they develop the ability, they recognise that as nothing has been added or subtracted the glasses must both contain the same amount regardless of appearance.

CONSERVATION OF NUMBER

The ability to conserve number was also tested by presenting the child with rows of coins.

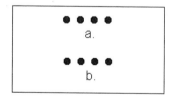

Question
Which row contains more coins? Or are they both the same?
Answer
Both the same.

Then the coins are rearranged.

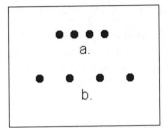

Question
Which row contains more coins?
Or are they both the same?
Answer
(Before ability to conserve) **Row b**
has more.
(After ability to conserve) **Both the same.**

Again the first child judges by appearance but the second has recognised that the amount is unaltered.

In order to be able to conserve the child must understand **compensation**. That is, that in the first example glass b's height is compensated by glass a's width. Piaget stated that children in the pre-operational stage couldn't compensate, understand reversibility or conservation.

They must also understand the concept of **reversibility** – physical actions and mental operations can be reversed. That is, just as you can spread the coins out, so you can put them back into their original sequence. Therefore, the number must be the same.

Table 2.2 Summary of the main characteristics of the pre-operational stage	
Egocentrism	Child can only view the world from their perspective and finds it difficult to understand any other perspective. (See Three Mountains Test)
Animism	The tendency to attribute feelings and intentions to inanimate objects – Teddy feels sad.
Conservation	Child is unable to complete conservation of volume, number, length, weight, liquid, area and mass. This is due to their inability to understand the concepts of compensation and reversibility.

The concrete operational stage (7–12 years)

The term **operations** is used because this stage is characterised by the development of strategies and rules for interpreting and investigating the child's world. The term **concrete** refers to the child's ability to apply these strategies to things that are present (Smith et al., 1998). Thus the child can solve problems they can see or manipulate.

Table 2.3 Summary of the main characteristics of the concrete operational stage	
Conservation	Child is able to complete conservation of volume, number, length, weight, liquid, area and mass by the end of the stage.
Inductive logic	Child begins to use own experience to develop principles/rules, which are then applied to immediate problem e.g. if I eat a sweet the number of sweets reduces – therefore each time I take something away the number I am left with is always smaller than the number I started with.
Class inclusion	Child recognises that categories include smaller sub-groups which are all part of the bigger category e.g. animal includes all cats and dogs, and dogs includes spaniels, Dobermans etc. but all dogs are included in the general class of animal.
Egocentricity	Diminishes in this stage

The formal operational stage (12–16 years)

The dependency on concrete objects diminishes in this stage and children are able to solve hypothetical problems or imagined problems that they are unable to see. This stage is characterised by the use of hypothetical deductive reasoning and systematic problem solving.

Hypothetical deductive reasoning is reasoning that uses deductive logic – e.g. a child is told that all rabbits have furry feet and all guinea pigs have bald feet. They are asked the question, What type of feet does my rabbit Lucy have? They will deduce that if all rabbits have furry feet and Lucy is a rabbit, she must have furry feet. This type of reasoning is not seen in younger children.

The second element of this stage is **systematic problem solving**. As the term suggests, a child at this stage will solve problems in a systematic and logical manner. For example, a child trying to make the colour purple from a set of paints will make a series of different combinations of colours but each new combination will be made on the basis of what they have learned from previous combinations. This is a systematic approach which will eventually solve the problem – it is not random but clearly thought out.

Table 2.4 Summary of the main characteristics of the formal operational stage	
Hypothetical deductive reasoning	This is reasoning that uses deductive logic. This type of reasoning is not seen in younger children.
Systematic problem solving	Child solves problems in a systematic manner.

Summary of Piaget's stage model of cognitive development

This chapter has presented Piaget's model of cognitive development and has detailed the main characteristics of each stage. To review this model, Table 2.5 presents a summary of each of the stages.

1. What is the sensorimotor stage of development?
2. What is egocentrism? Why does egocentrism affect children's ability to solve problems such as the Three Mountains Task?
3. Why can children in the concrete operational period conserve? What are reversibility and compensation?
4. How do children in the formal operational stage solve problems?

Progress exercise

Table 2.5 Summary of Piaget's stage model of cognitive development

Stage	Summary
Sensorimotor stage 0–2 years	<ul><li>Child uses sensory and motor skills to explore and gain understanding of their world.</li><li>Their knowledge is limited and based on physical experiences.</li><li>As mobility increases so does the ability to explore and therefore develop cognitive abilities.</li><li>This stage is divided into six sub-stages in which each stage builds on the previous one.</li></ul>
Pre-operational stage 2–7 years	<ul><li>This stage is divided into two sub-stages – the pre-conceptual period and the intuitive period.</li><li>During this stage children begin to use symbols and respond to objects and events.</li><li>Egocentrism is a key characteristic – viewing the world from the child's perspective and the inability to use the perspective of others.</li><li>Animism – attributing feeling and intentions to inanimate objects, part of pre-conceptual stage.</li><li>Inability to conserve.</li><li>Thinking is not logical or reversible.</li></ul>
Concrete operational stage 7–12 years	<ul><li>Children understand reversibility and compensation.</li><li>By the end of the stage children can conserve.</li><li>Egocentric thought diminishes.</li><li>Principles of class inclusion are understood.</li><li>General principles are developed and applied to immediate problems through inductive knowledge.</li></ul>

continued . . .

Table 2.5 *continued*	
Stage	Summary
Formal operational stage 12–16 years	• Children use hypothetical deductive reasoning to solve problems. Concrete objects no longer required. • Children use a systematic approach to problem solving. • The ability to think in an abstract manner occurs at this stage.

Empirical evidence and evaluation

This far we have examined Piaget's stage theory and detailed the key characteristics of each stage. It is necessary to evaluate this theory and therefore this discussion will now draw upon empirical studies to provide this evaluation. Each topic will be examined and a discussion of the empirical evidence in support of and in critique of Piaget will be detailed.

Object permanence

In support of Piaget

Piaget found that children were unable to achieve object permanence before 8 months of age – he noted that once an object was removed from the field of vision, babies below this age stopped looking for it.

In opposition to Piaget

Bower (1982) found that babies less than 4 months of age showed signs of object permanence. Babies were shown a toy and then a screen was placed in front of it. When the screen was removed for half the babies the toy was still there, for the other half the toy had been taken away. The babies in the second group showed more surprise when the screen was removed, suggesting that they still expected the toy to be there – showing they had object permanence.

Ballargeon and Devos (1991) showed 3–4-month-old babies a carrot on a truck – there was a large and a small carrot. The trucks passed behind a window – babies looked for longer when the large carrot went behind the window, suggesting that they expected to be able to see it above the window-sill – they had achieved object permanence. They knew that they should be able to see the carrot when the truck went past the window, as it was big enough to show above the window-sill.

Luo, Baillargeon, Brueckner and Munakata (2003) also support the notion that young babies have object permanence. In their study they found signs of object permanence in 5-month-old babies.

Egocentrism

In support of Piaget

Piaget and Inhelder tested children on the Three Mountains Task; they found that by the age of 9 all children were able to successfully complete the task.

Brewer (2001) provided children with a piggy bank – the money was taken out and replaced with marbles in front of the children. Then the children were asked what other people would *think* was in the bank. Younger children showed egocentricity by answering 'marbles'. Older children were able to answer 'money'. They were able to see the piggy bank from another perspective – although they knew it contained marbles, they understood that other people would have a different point of view and assume that, as it was a piggy bank, it contained money.

In opposition to Piaget

Bell et al. (1975) found that children were able to complete the Three Mountains Task at an earlier age than Piaget stated if the characters used were a doll and a policeman and the doll was hiding from the policeman. This may be because this scenario is more natural for children and they are able to identify with it as a game. This suggests that Piaget's idea about egocentrism in young children may be flawed and his results may have been due to his own test design (see later for a discussion of Piaget's design).

Brewer (2001) observed 3-year-old children engaging in pretend play. She stated that this illustrated their lack of egocentrism, as they were able to act as another individual and therefore must be able to use more than one perspective. Role play frequently observed in pre-school children would contradict Piaget's notions of egocentrism.

McDonald and Stuart-Hamilton (2003) conducted a repeat of the Three Mountains Task with adults and found that even adults, whom Piaget would consider non-egocentric participants, made mistakes. They argue that the task is too difficult even for some adults. Therefore children's inability to complete the task may be more to do with the design than with their ability.

Animism

In support of Piaget

Piaget found evidence of animism in children in the pre-operational period.

In opposition to Piaget

Carey (1985) found that few children at kindergarten (nursery) still showed signs of animism, suggesting that they stopped attributing feelings to inanimate objects before Piaget suggested and showing that children in this stage can distinguish between objects which are alive and those which are not.

Conservation

In opposition to Piaget

McGarrigle and Donaldson (1974) introduced a naughty teddy into the conservation experiments. The teddy accidentally messed up the experiment, for example the teddy accidentally moved the coins and then children had to determine if there were still the same number of coins, now that the teddy had messed the row up and it looked different. The researchers found that children were able to answer the conservation tests correctly at an earlier age in these conditions.

Rose and Blank (1974) and Samuel and Bryant (1984) suggested that children are confused by the questions and not the task. They are asked if there is more in A or B, and then asked the same question again after the experiment has been rearranged. It was felt that if children were asked the same question twice, they would assume that they had answered incorrectly the first time and therefore answer differently. When only one question is asked this leads to a better performance, although there are still age differences.

Houdee and Guichart (2001) suggest that the conservation tasks do not measure children's ability to understand underlying logic, but are a measure of their ability to deal with the interference introduced by the tasks.

In support of Piaget

Piaget conducted his conservation experiments and found that children below the concrete operational stage were unable to conserve.

Moore and Frye (1986) suggested that the introduction of the 'naughty teddy' discussed above did not demonstrate that children could conserve at an earlier age than Piaget specified. They suggested that the teddy distracted the children and then they concentrated on the teddy and not the experiment. Therefore they were unaware that changes had taken place, and this was why they answered correctly and seemed to be able to conserve. They simply didn't realise changes had taken place, as they were not watching.

Concrete operational stage

In support of Piaget

Eysink, Dijkstra and Kuper (2001) supported Piaget's theory of the development of knowledge and concepts from interaction with the objects in a recent study involving students solving computer problems. Students who struggled to solve the problems were more successful when they were able to draw out pictures of the problems and then to solve them.

Formal operational stage

In support of Piaget

Piaget and Inhelder (1956) presented children with the four-beaker problem. Four beakers were filled with odourless and colourless liquid. The children had to work out which combination of liquids turned yellow. Piaget and Inhelder found that children in the concrete operational stage used a random problem-solving technique but children in the formal operational stage used a systematic approach. This was further supported by the pendulum task where individuals had to work out which length of string and which weight would affect the speed of the pendulum swing – again children in the concrete operational stage used a random approach whereas children in the formal stage used a systematic approach. (For a more detailed discussion of this study see Chapter 6 Study Aids.)

In opposition to Piaget

Bryant and Trabasso (1971) suggested that failure to complete such complex tasks as the beaker and pendulum tasks was due to memory failure – children were not able to remember what solutions they had tried. They found that if children were trained they could solve more complex problems. This suggests that children may have the cognitive ability to solve the tasks but that their ability is limited by their memory. It may be that children require training and advice in how to use their knowledge to enter the formal operational stage.

Sutherland (1982) stated that 50% of 16 year olds are still at the concrete operational stage or even at a lower stage. He also stated that it could not be assumed that adults had reached the formal operational stage, even when they entered higher education. This suggests that support for the existence of the formal operational stage, and certainly the timing of it, is questionable.

Language and social factors

In support of Piaget

Linguistic training (see below) did not improve ability to solve the conservation tasks; this suggests that Piaget had correctly identified a developmental stage.

In opposition to Piaget

Sinclair-de-Zwart (1969) stated that children's inability to conserve was linked to language development. Children who had broader vocabularies were able to complete the tasks. If children used words like 'smaller than' or 'biggest' rather than 'big' and 'little' they were more likely to be able to solve the conservation tasks. Thus conservation may depend on language development – which is linked to cognitive development

Although there is a significant degree of criticism of Piaget's original theory, aspects of it have been supported. Piaget's idea that the child is an active learner and his notion of the importance of learning through doing – the little scientist; behaviour shaping thinking – have been supported. Also the notion of development in cognitive thinking has also been seen to have support within this chapter. All of these issues are incorporated in Piaget's views of education and the educational implications of his theory.

Educational implications of Piaget's theory

It is important when evaluating Piaget's theory to consider not only the empirical studies but also the great impact that Piaget had upon education. Although aspects of his theory have been critiqued it is important to note that he had a vast impact on the education of children especially primary age children. Piaget's work heavily influenced educational theories and practice.

The role of the teacher

Until Piaget, the teacher's role was that of an individual who imparted knowledge, and the child was a passive recipient of this knowledge.

Piaget introduced child-centred learning. It was his view that children differed from adults in the manner in which they acquired knowledge. Therefore, teaching has to be focused upon the child, taking into account their developmental stage and level. Piaget felt that the child should not have free will over their learning, but learning should be teacher-directed. The teacher initiates and determines the activities. The role of the teacher is to create a situation in which the child can learn and to encourage questions, experiments and speculation (Slavin, 1994).

Readiness

As Piaget thought that cognitive development occurs in stages, he thought that children needed to be cognitively ready to learn new concepts. He thought that it was of no use to try and encourage a child to engage in a task which was beyond their level of cognitive development. He would suggest that asking a child in the pre-operational stage to attempt a task requiring compensation was inappropriate because they are not ready to engage in such a task. Teachers therefore need to be aware of the child's level of development in order to set appropriate tasks. Tasks which are beyond the child's level of development are likely to lead to failure and de-motivation.

Active learning

Piaget did not think that children simply absorb knowledge. He thought that they learnt by being actively involved in the process. Therefore good learning requires participation. Active involvement leads to a greater sense of interest and understanding. For example, a child may be told that if you freeze water it turns to ice. This may be a difficult idea to understand. If they fill an ice cube tray, place it in the freezer and later return to see the changes that have occurred, they are likely to have a much clearer understanding. Education, Piaget felt, needed to be about much more than just listening to a teacher. He felt that children learn by doing. The child, according to Piaget, is a natural scientist and explorer, and needs to be provided with opportunities to learn by actively using these natural abilities (Slavin, 1994).

Holton, Ahmed, Williams and Hill (2001) illustrated the importance of active learning and play even in maths learning. They suggest the importance of play in providing opportunity to learn and try. They see play as a basis for mathematical learning in children. This illustrates the importance of play and active learning even in subjects seen as more traditional.

The role of active learning was further emphasised by Sutherland (1999) who suggested that individuals need a practical element to their learning until they have reached the formal operational stage. As we are now unsure when this is achieved, Sutherland suggests that even in higher education teachers need to allow the opportunity for active learning.

Learning from mistakes

Piaget thought that teaching should focus on the child's reasoning, therefore an incorrect answer is as valuable as a correct one, as it can be used to identify the child's reasoning and therefore to teach general principles. For example, if Jack answers that 8 times itself is 16, he has multiplied 8 by 2 (i.e. 2 lots of 8). There is logic here and by discussing the incorrect answer the notion of a square number can be taught (Slavin, 1994).

Peer interaction

Piaget considered socialisation to be an important part of education. Through peer interaction, ideas can be developed and challenged. This type of interaction requires children to consider another viewpoint. Interaction with peers challenges thinking, as peers are on a similar cognitive level (Birch, 1998).

Use of real materials

Children below the formal operational stage cannot solve problems in an abstract manner. They will achieve more by solving problems using actual materials. For example, children trying to understand which objects will float and which will sink may not be able to identify them from a list of objects. However, if they have the materials and place them in a bucket of water they will learn the properties of objects which float. Similarly if children are trying to learn to count in 3s they may find this difficult to do in their heads. If they have a series of counters which they can place into groups of 3, they will be able to work out the answer to 3 times 3. (Birch, 1998; Woolfolk & McCune-Nicolich, 1984)

New concepts

Children need new concepts and new learning to be linked to previous knowledge in order that they can assimilate and accommodate this new information. For example, if a teacher wished to teach her children the 4 times table she could link this to the 3 times table they have already learned by providing the children with the same counters and getting them to put them in groups of 4 (Birch, 1998).

Other issues

Although Piaget's work was extremely influential it has been heavily criticised. Some of these criticisms are discussed below.

Age

Piaget seems to have underestimated the cognitive abilities of young children and overestimated the cognitive abilities of older children. Bower (1982) investigated the ability of babies aged 5–6 months and found that they showed evidence of object permanence. Pramling and Samuelsson (2001) suggest that 3-year-old children can solve basic science problems if they are presented correctly. In their experiment such children were capable of solving elementary physics problems if they were clearly explained by the teacher. This suggests that Piaget had indeed underestimated the abilities of young children.

Earlier in this chapter the work of Sutherland (1982) was reviewed which showed that only 50% of children displayed formal operations at the expected age. These problems have led some psychologists to suggest that although Piaget's stages may exist, the ages that are attached to them need to be reconsidered.

Questions used

Piaget's tests and tasks have been criticised for using language that is unfamiliar to the child or for asking questions in a difficult or awkward manner. Donaldson (1978) looked at the language used in Piaget's *class inclusion* tests. The language and questions were found to be confusing. When questions were rephrased the number of correct responses rose from 25% to 48%. Earlier in this chapter the work of Samuel and Bryant was discussed. Their work showed that the questions asked in the conservation experiments were often very confusing to children, and that if only one question was asked the number of correct responses increased.

Test design

Piaget's experiments used materials and scenarios that were unfamiliar to the child, and often the way tasks were presented produced problems. Experiments using sweets for conservation of number have found conservation at younger ages than Piaget specified. McGarrigle and Donaldson (1974) introduced a 'naughty teddy' into the conservation tests and this change to the design resulted in 70% of 4–6 year olds being able to conserve.

When the Three Mountains Test is produced in a different way (Bell et al., 1975; see earlier) children are able to complete the task at earlier ages. Recent research illustrated the interesting point that adults found the task difficult to complete, and that they were forced into making errors by the design when in fact they were non-egocentric participants (McDonald & Stuart-Hamilton, 2003).

Light, Buckingham and Robbins (1979) conducted a different version of the conservation task by having two identical beakers containing food, and then showing children that one beaker had a chip. The children were then told to put the food from that beaker into a different-shaped beaker so that it was safe. Under these conditions more children were able to state that the amount of food remained the same, even though it now looked different. This suggests that the way in which the conservation test is designed may be the reason for children's failure and not their inability to conserve.

Language

Frank (1966) claimed that language could help to overcome concrete thinking. However, as we have seen, Sinclair-de-Zwart (1969) found no evidence that language training improved performance.

Practice

If the development of cognition is related to maturity – i.e. that certain abilities are only possible at certain ages – then practice will not improve performance. Danner and Day (1977) did find improvement in formal operational problem-solving performance after practice but the most obvious improvement was in older children. This suggests that maturity does have an effect.

Summary of evaluative points

Piaget developed the first comprehensive account of children's cognitive development. His work challenged the passive view of the child and led to a vast amount of research. Piaget developed a stage theory of cognitive development. Each stage represents a development in thinking and understanding. This theory consists of the sensorimotor stage, the pre-operational stage, the concrete operational stage and the formal operational stage. He developed the Three Mountains Task and tests of conservation to investigate children's cognitive development. Piaget's theory had great educational implications and a real impact on education, especially primary education.

Although Piaget's work was extremely significant and changed the way in which children's thinking was perceived, there have been criticisms of his work. There seems to be an underestimation of early ability and an overestimation of later stages. Piaget often used small samples and has been accused of bias. This has led to claims that his experiments lacked academic rigour. Piaget was aware of some of the limitations of his model and theory, and continued to critique and revise it through his life. Some supporters of Piaget state that the problem is in using the model too strictly and that it should only be used as a guide.

Some of the criticisms of Piaget's work have led to the development of other theories. A major alternative theory to that of Piaget is the theory developed by Vygotsky. This theory will be discussed and evaluated in the next chapter.

Review exercise

In what ways may Piaget have underestimated children's abilities?

What other criticisms of Piaget's theory have been made?

What research and evidence could be used to support these criticisms?

Further reading

Smith, P.K., Cowie, H. & Blades, M. (1998) *Understanding Children's Development* (3rd Edition), Blackwell. Chapter 11 provides a detailed account of Piaget. There is probably too much detail for A-level demands, but it is a source of further information.

Brewer, S. (2001) *A Child's World*, Headline Publishing Company, Ch. 4 'The Thinker'. This is not necessarily an academic text, but it provides illustrations and accounts of the development of thinking in children.

3

Vygotsky's theory of cognitive development

Introduction

Lev Vygotsky (1896–1934) was a Russian and a student of literature, law and cultural studies. Much of his work, which has been very influential, was not published in English until after his death. Vygotsky agreed with Piaget that a child does not sit back and somehow passively absorb knowledge but instead actively constructs knowledge. This idea was in direct contrast to the view of Pavlov that learning was essentially a passive activity. However, Vygotsky's theory differs in key principles from Piaget. He stated that children's complex thinking was acquired through social interactions between children and the adults around them. The child will interact with others – peers, parents and teachers – and these interactions will result in learning.

Vygotsky's theory

Vygotsky's theory focused upon three key factors. These were culture, language and the zone of proximal development.

Culture

Vygotsky thought that the culture and social environment of the child was a vital part of their construction of knowledge (see Figure 3.1). That is, that what children learn about the world and the way this knowledge is learned is determined by the society to which they belong and the social settings they are part of. The child learns through interactions with others but also through elements of their own culture, for example songs, language, art and play. For instance a child who grows up in a predominantly Catholic country may encounter, through language and society, strong anti-abortion views. This will affect his or her learning, knowledge and viewpoint on this issue.

To summarise, Vygotsky stated that first culture affects learning, as children learn through interactions and cooperation with others and the environment, and second the child develops through the **symbolic representations** of the child's culture, i.e. art, language, play, songs etc. The child's development both reflects and internalises the culture to which they belong. Therefore, the culture provides a framework in which the child constructs meaning.

Language

Vygotsky saw language as of central importance in the learning process. He thought that there was a clear relationship between language development and cognitive development. Vygotsky thought that we encode and represent our world through language, that language is a

Figure 3.1 **The interaction between culture and development**

symbolic system by which we communicate and that language is a
cultural tool.

Stages of language development

Vygotsky stated that there were three stages of language development. These are described in Table 3.1, based on Luna (1992) and
LeFrancois (1994).

Table 3.1 Vygotsky's stages of language development		
Stage	**Approx. Age**	**Description**
Social speech (external speech)	Up to 3 years	Speech is used to control the behaviour of others. Express simple thoughts and emotions e.g. I want daddy. This provokes behaviour – getting daddy.
Egocentric speech	3–7 years	Children talk to themselves regardless of other individuals who are listening. They say things out loud to guide their behaviour. They talk about what they are doing and why. Their reasoning is that language must be spoken to direct behaviour, e.g. a child will often say hop, scotch, hop when playing a game of hopscotch as if to tell their body what to do.
Inner speech	7+ and adults	This inner speech is silent; it is used to direct behaviour or thoughts. When this stage is reached individuals can engage in all types of higher mental functions. An adult may have an inner conversation about what to cook for dinner or what they will say when they meet someone. This prepares them and directs behaviour in the actual situation.

Language and thought

Vygotsky stated that language was an important part of cognitive development. An important question concerns the relationship between language and thought – what comes first, language or thought, and what is the relationship between them? Do we need language in order to be able to understand our thoughts, or do we need thoughts to understand what language means? Vygotsky felt that language was necessary for an individual to organise their thought. He placed more emphasis on the importance of language development than Piaget did.

Vygotsky's theory suggested that at first language and thought are separate processes. Young children's language and thinking are both basic and not yet developed. Initially language is used for social purposes and is not connected to inner thoughts. Vygotsky stated that by the age of 2 language and thought become related and language starts to have a major influence on cognitive and social development. Vygotsky suggested that from the age of 2 cognitive development was at least partly controlled by language.

Vygotsky thought that the development of language was possible because of culture. The learning of language is made possible through social processes and the influence of culture. As a child develops and matures their thought processes become more developed and more mature, as does their use and understanding of language. Vygotsky saw a definite relationship between language and thought. Language, Vygotsky also thought, directed behaviour (LeFrancois, 1994). Vygotsky saw cognitive development as deriving from conversation with parents and others, and dialogue with the wider society (Smith et al., 1998).

Elementary and higher mental functions

Vygotsky made a distinction between elementary and higher mental functions. **Elementary mental functions** are natural and unlearned behaviours, i.e. sensation. We can develop these to some extent through experience. **Higher mental functions** are aspects which need to be developed through learning, i.e. language and memory, thinking, paying attention etc. Inner speech is required for higher mental functions. We need culture and inner speech to transform elementary mental functions to higher mental functions. Culture is transmitted through language and the help of 'expert others' (see below).

The zone of proximal development

A key factor of Vygotsky's theory was the concept of the **zone of proximal development** or ZPD. The idea was that at any point in time a child is functioning at a particular level of development. However, Vygotsky thought that each child was capable of further development if supported and guided by experienced others.

The zone of proximal development or ZPD is the distance between the actual developmental level and the potential level of the child. There is a contrast between the actual level, which includes processes that are already developed, and the ZPD, which includes processes / functions that are not mature yet (see Figure 3.2).

A key factor in this theory is the role of the teacher or experienced **expert other**. Vygotsky's idea was that the teacher or experienced other provides a vital role in guiding the child, making suggestions, offering strategies. A young child might struggle to complete a 25-piece jigsaw, but an adult working with them might suggest strategies such as turning pieces round, making the edge first or trying to put together pieces of the same colour. In this way the child makes use of the more expert other's knowledge, but it is the child who completes the jigsaw. They are able to achieve something which is not in their own levels of capability. Thus they move from their actual level to their potential level. The child is not a scientist trying out solutions but is an active learner guided by experienced others. These others can help the child's development and enhance their achievements.

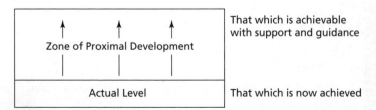

Figure 3.2 **The zone of proximal development**

Scaffolding

Bruner developed Vygotsky's ideas further. He suggested that the more expert individual provides **scaffolding** for the learner. The adult provides a framework or scaffold while the child develops their understanding. At first the adult may need to give many suggestions and prompts. These will decrease as they are no longer needed. If we return to the earlier example, when the child first completes such jigsaws much help and guidance is required. As the child practises they learn strategies such as making the edge first and therefore the adult needs to provide less support and fewer verbal prompts.

Unlike Piaget, Vygotsky did not think children needed to be ready to learn new concepts but that they should be provided with problems above their level of development. These activities will promote learning if it is scaffolded and if it falls within the ZPD. If the activity is beyond the ZPD the child will fail and be unable to understand the strategies and solutions needed to solve the problem. This could have a negative effect on the child and their future attempts at learning. Thus the more experienced partner provides help by being an intellectual scaffold, which allows the less expert learner to achieve more difficult tasks than may be possible alone (Stone, 1995).

This scaffolding, Bruner suggested, is necessary in learning new concepts. For example, when a child is learning to multiply, a sum of 6×2 may be impossible, but the expert may suggest starting with 2 then adding 2 until they reach 6 lots of 2. This provides the child with a strategy to solve this and future problems. Just as in any building work, a scaffold is not permanently required – once the concept is understood the scaffold can be removed and the child will be able to solve the problem unaided.

Progress exercise

Write a brief answer to the questions below.

1. What are the key factors which Vygotsky thought influenced cognitive development?

2. What is the zone of proximal development? How can more expert others help children's development?

Vygotsky's stage model of concept formation

Vygotsky constructed a model, which described the development of children's concept formation. A diagram of this model can be seen in Figure 3.3.

Vygotsky (1987) presented children with wooden blocks, which differed in shape and height. Each block was labelled with a nonsense syllable. The children were asked to work out what the syllables meant. He noted that they worked through the first three stages seen in Figure 3.3 before achieving mature concepts. In the first stage children largely form concepts by trial and error. During the second stage they use some appropriate strategies but they do not identify the main attributes. In the third stage children identified only one attribute at a time. Finally children were able to process several different attributes at the same time.

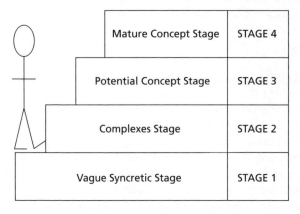

Figure 3.3 Vygotsky's stage model of concept formation

Evaluation

It must be noted that Vygotsky's theory has not been tested as broadly as Piaget's theory. Piaget's theory is relatively easy to test, as it is possible to replicate his studies and to scientifically investigate his ideas through experiments. However, Vygotsky's ideas cannot be tested in this way because the factors that he identified as important, such as culture, are not easily testable. However, there is some empirical evidence and this will now be reviewed.

In support of Vygotsky

Higher mental functions

Gredler (1992) stated that if higher mental functions depend on cultural influences then we should find different higher mental functions in different cultures. He supported this with evidence that in Papua New Guinea children use a counting system that begins on one thumb and goes up the arm and down to the other fingers, ending at number 29. This culturally determined system makes the higher function of adding and subtracting difficult. This demonstrates differences due to culture.

Stage model of concept formation

Crawford (2001) suggests that Vygotsky's model of concept development is a model for understanding the development of moral ability, and suggests similar stages in the development of moral ability.

Expert others

Fruend (1990) arranged for one group of children to play by themselves with a doll's house and for another group to play with their mother (the expert other). When the children were asked to complete a furniture-sorting task, those who had worked with their mother earlier showed a dramatic improvement in their ability to complete the task. This provided support for the roles of the expert other in helping children develop from their current level to their potential level, and the role of the expert other in scaffolding learning.

More recent computer tutorials have been based upon Vygotsky's model. Children complete tests on the computer until they are unable to answer a question and then they switch to a tutorial to guide them through the problem. The computer records exactly what type of help and how much help is given. Thus the children can all work at their own levels but make use of the more expert other when required (Hippisley, 2001). This has improved individual learning.

Peers can also be seen as experts. Blaye et al. (1991) investigated co-working in computer games. The task of the 11-year-old children was to solve problems presented in a computer game. Some of the children worked alone and others in pairs. The tasks were very difficult and no individuals completed them successfully, and only some of the pairs were successful. In the second session there was some improvement – 50% of pairs were successful as opposed to less than 20% of individuals. In the third session all children worked on their own. Over 70% of children who had previously worked in pairs were successful, compared to 30% of children who had previously worked alone (Cardwell et al., 2000; 458). The suggestion is that the discussions between the pairs had enhanced their development through the ZPD and thus they benefited from peer tutoring. Further evidence for peer tutoring comes from Bennet and Dunne (1991). They found that children who worked together were less competitive and more likely to produce logical thinking than those working alone.

Hooper and Walker (2002) conducted a longitudinal study on the effect of peer tutoring on the communication skills of those learning Makaton (a sign language). They investigated 126 tutors working in 23 different establishments and found evidence for the positive impact of peer tutoring – 16 establishments noted that student communication skills had increased, but importantly the peer tutoring had also resulted in increases in self-esteem and confidence. Clearly this research supports Vygotsky's idea about the importance of peer tutoring.

The use of peer instruction has been found to have a positive impact on the learning of introductory physics by university students. Researchers compared two groups of students, one group whose learning was supported by teacher-guided notes and the other whose learning was supported by peer instruction. They found a positive impact on learning for students who had peer instruction (Lenaerts, Wieme & Zele, 2003).

Levels of speech

Support for the three levels of language described by Vygotsky is provided by Prior and Welling (2001). They demonstrated the progression from egocentric speech to inner speech. In their study they conducted comprehension tests on a group of 73 pupils from Grades

2, 3 and 4. The pupils were given comprehension tests after silent and oral reading of passages. The researchers used different texts to reflect the different ages of the children. Children in Grade 2 showed no difference in their comprehension of the texts whether they had read them silently or out loud. However, children in Grades 3 and 4 showed a significantly higher score after oral reading as opposed to silent reading. This study provides support for Vygotsky's notion of progression from egocentric to inner speech, as the younger children had a clearer understanding when reading aloud.

ZPD

Recently the importance of the ZPD has been emphasised, not just in children's education but also in further and higher education. Hasse found that students could be encouraged to reach their creative potential if they were supported by more expert staff and if their potential level of development was equal to the actual level of development of staff members. If their potential level of development fell below the actual level of development of staff, then students were unlikely to reach their creative potential (Hasse, 2001). Harland (2003) describes the use of the ZPD in teaching in higher education and stresses the importance of staff knowledge of the ZPD in promoting student learning. This supports the value of the ZPD and shows it has a practical educational implication.

Scaffolding

McNaughton and Leyland (1990) provided support for the idea of scaffolding and demonstrated that this had different stages related to task difficulty. When the child was working on puzzles which were too easy (below the ZPD) the mother's approach was just to keep the child focused on the task. At the next level of difficulty (within the ZPD) the mother's approach was to encourage and help the child to solve the puzzle independently. When the puzzle was too hard (beyond the ZPD) the mother helped the child complete the task by any method, recognising that it was too difficult. Scaffolding was evident throughout the experiment.

The importance of the use of scaffolding within computer packages for on-line learning has been recognised (Sims, Dobbs & Hand, 2002).

Recently there has been the introduction of interactive computer toys, which suggest hints and strategies for young children learning to use the computer – this is an example of scaffolding in practice without the need for a real life expert other (Luckin, Connolly, Plowman, & Airey, 2003). It also illustrates the broad application of Vygotsky's theory that is possible.

In opposition to Vygotsky

Oppositions of Vygotsky's theory have tended to be quite general; three arguments against Vygotsky are listed below.

Expert others

Vygotsky assumed that the ZPD illustrates the development possible when intervention occurs from a more expert other. However, this theory does not take into account the quality of the help given, and assumes that if help is given it is always the same type and degree of help. In addition, children often learn from other children who are working at the same level as themselves.

Cost

The type of intervention Vygotsky promotes is very time-consuming and may not be appropriate or possible in the current educational system, especially as class sizes are increasing and there is a problem with teacher recruitment. Teachers need to be aware of each individual child's level of development and then plan tasks to help them reach their potential level – providing the necessary staff to do this is seen to be a problem. In addition the current emphasis on SATs may make implementing Vygotsky's theory difficult. Also this theory may require staff to be retrained.

Peer tutoring

Blaye et al. (1991) conducted a study that seemed to provide support for the role of peer tutoring. However, not all the children who worked in pairs were successful and some individuals did succeed, although working together produced a greater degree of success generally than working alone. Factors such as group status and individual ability seem influential. Children of higher status and greater ability benefit most from peer tutoring. This demonstrates the limitations of peer tutoring.

Educational implications of Vygotsky's theory

Vygotsky's theory, like Piaget's, had educational implications. His theory led to ideas about the way in which education should be structured.

Culture

Vygotsky argued for the importance of culture. This has implications for education in that it has been argued that tests of attainment need to take account of the social context of the child and not just their score. For example, if we use Vygotsky's model we can see that a child in a school that offers stimulation and access to a more expert other, is in a better position than a child in a school that does not. Children with access to a more expert other may use the expert to help them develop new strategies and techniques, and therefore to encourage their cognitive development. When children are tested for their SATs they are given a score. This score takes no account of the social environment of the child. Vygotsky would argue that the environment is extremely important in cognitive development, and therefore comparing all children using the same tests without taking account of the environment may produce results which provide an inaccurate picture of the child's abilities. What is really being measured is their educational environment and not their ability.

Language

As language is seen to be of such importance to Vygotsky, it is suggested that education should offer many opportunities for the use of and development of language. Children need to be encouraged to listen and to discuss ideas with other peers and teachers. By discussion and use of language, children can be encouraged to move from their current ideas to more developed ideas. Through discussion children can ask questions and come to a full understanding of new ideas. As Vygotsky stated that there was a clear relationship between language and thought, he would argue that discussion of ideas leads to a greater understanding.

ZPD

Perhaps the most important implication of Vygotsky's work is the role it suggested for the teacher. Teaching should be based upon the child's level of development and potential development. The teacher should be aware that the child learns through his or her own exploration. The teacher needs to be aware of the individual child's levels of competence when structuring teaching. The child should be given tasks which encourage them to reach their potential level of development. If the tasks are too easy they will not encourage new thinking or development. If they are beyond the child's ZPD the child will fail and this can have a negative impact on future learning. It is therefore important that the teacher is aware of the child's ZPD and sets tasks which are difficult enough to encourage the child's learning. However, the teacher must be available to scaffold this new learning.

The expert other

Vygotsky introduced the concept of the expert other. He argued that adult intervention in education is important. The teacher can guide and work with the child to develop strategies and solve puzzles. Therefore having intervention from an individual who knows the answer is positive. The individual can judge the amount of support or guidance that is required. Little help may be required on some tasks and more on others, and the child benefits from the experience of the more expert individual. Teachers should offer opportunities for children to develop skills and understanding through interaction with other children, but particularly with more expert others. These may be teachers or indeed more experienced peers or parents.

Peer tutoring

Vygotsky also promoted the use of collaborative learning or **peer mentoring**. Using older 'more expert' pupils to help and guide the work of younger less experienced children is common practice in many school environments. For example, young readers are assigned an older listener to hear them read. The older reader listens and helps when necessary, perhaps teaching new sounds or words. This then develops the younger child's reading skills.

Scaffolding

Scaffolding is a key part of education and can be seen in Table 3.2 to have different stages. Scaffolding is seen to be an important part of

Table 3.2 Stages of scaffolding according to Bruner	
Stage	**Description**
Recruitment	First the teacher must obtain the interest of the child and ensure they are actively engaged, and then encourage them to attempt the requirements of the task.
Reduction of degrees of freedom	The teacher needs to make the task simple by reducing the number of acts required to complete the task. The learner must be able to judge whether he or she has fulfilled the task requirements or not.
Direction maintenance	The teacher needs to maintain motivation in the child. First this will require active encouragement by the teacher, later the problem itself will provide the motivation for completion.
Marking critical features	A teacher focuses on the parts of the task that are the most relevant. This allows the child to compare their own results / work with correct results and investigate any discrepancies.
Demonstration	The adult provides a demonstration of completion of a task that is partly done by the child. The child should then imitate the learner's performance.

Based on Wood, Bruner, and Gross (1976) in Smith et al. (2001).

education. Children need teachers to offer support and frameworks for them to learn in, together with opportunities to build on previous experience.

Play

Vygotsky emphasised the importance of play as part of education. He saw play as important in that imagination and play stretch a child's conceptual ability and therefore lead to development. Play leads to a basic understanding of abstract thought. For example through play a child can learn new concepts such as big and little, tall and short. They can also learn about emotion and social issues through play. Play allows children to try out different kinds of behaviour and strategies within a safe environment. Children can then transfer knowledge and strategies developed through play to other problems and activities.

Summary of Vygotsky's theory

Vygotsky thought that children actively construct knowledge. He emphasised the importance of culture and language. Vygotsky thought that there were three stages of language development – social, ego-centric and inner speech. Vygotsky stated that culture was needed to move from elementary mental functions to higher mental functions. A main focus of his theory was the ZPD. He thought that scaffolding of learning was important, as was the educational role of the expert other. The empirical evidence for Vygotsky is growing and provides support for higher mental functions, the role of the expert other, peer function, levels of speech, the ZPD and scaffolding. Criticisms are general but include the fact that the intervention Vygotsky suggested is costly and time-consuming, not all children benefit from peer tutoring, and it is flawed to assume equality of help from an expert other. Vygotsky's work had many educational implications including the role of the teacher, collaborative learning, scaffolding, the impor-tance of culture and play, and language development. Vygotsky's theory was and is very influential in the field of cognitive development.

Review exercise

Select three of the most important features of Vygotsky's theory and suggest how each can be applied in teaching.

A comparison between the theories of Piaget and Vygotsky

Piaget	Vygotsky
Both agree that children are active learners.	
Thinking develops in recognisable stages which are dependent upon natural maturation.	The development of thinking is dependent upon language and culture.
The role of the teacher is seen as important but the use of a more-expert other is not a central concept of this theory.	The use of a more-expert other is seen as a fundamental part of children's cognitive development.
Readiness is a central concept of education. Children need to be cognitively ready to progress in their learning.	Children should be actively encouraged to move through their ZPD. Children do not need to be ready to progress but should be given opportunities to engage in problems beyond the current level of ability but within their ZPD.
Scaffolding is not a concept in this theory.	Scaffolding is a central concept in this theory.

continued . . .

| This theory was very influential in education but has required revisions, and the underestimation of children's abilities is still a problem. | This theory is currently very influential in education. |

Information processing approaches (IPA)

An alternative way to explain cognitive development is the information processing approach (IPA). Children are still seen as active processors of information, as with the theories of Piaget and Vygotsky. However, in contrast to these theories, the IPA does not attempt to provide an explanation for every aspect of children's thinking at every stage, but rather to investigate the processes used to interpret, store, retrieve and evaluate information. The IPA suggests that information is changed and structured by the brain.

The key idea of this theory is that the brain is viewed as a computer, which processes information. The 'hardware' can be thought of as the nerves and tissues, and the 'software' or 'programs' as the processes which occur during cognition. Thus the child can be seen to be an information processor. As you will be aware, computers are not all the same – some run faster and more efficiently than others. Computers with a higher specification are more efficient and effective than computers with a lower specification. A key idea of the IPA is that young children are like the lower-specification computers and are less efficient at processing, storing and retrieving information, but as they develop and mature they become much better information processors and therefore are able to complete cognitive tasks more efficiently and effectively.

The IPA includes a consideration of memory and attention. The IPA usually explains cognitive development as a gradual and continuous process of development and not a stage model. Important things to consider in the IPA are the limitations of the processing system and the strategies used to improve processing.

A key researcher in this field is Case (1985). Case used the term **M-space** to refer to the working memory or mental space available to the child. M-space can be loosely thought of as working memory. (For more information on the topic of memory, see the book entitled

Memory and Forgetting, also in this series.) This is where information is held while it is being worked on or processed. Obviously the bigger the amount of space available to work on problems and to input information the better. However, it is not just the amount of space that counts but also how it is used. Children's M-space will increase in their early years but will then reach its maximum. To make the best use of it and to be efficient at cognitive tasks, it then becomes a question of using it as effectively as possible.

Children use the M-space more effectively as they develop for a number of reasons. The first is that they do employ strategies to process information more effectively. At first these strategies are not automatic but as the child develops, the strategies become more and more automatic, so that they employ them without thinking about it.

Summary

The theories of Piaget and Vygotsky have been reviewed and evaluated. An alternative explanation to these theories has been offered through consideration of the IPA. So far, general principles of cognitive development have been discussed. The following chapters will focus upon two distinct aspects of cognitive development, these being the development of measured intelligence and the development of moral understanding.

Further reading

Smith, P.K., Cowie, H. & Blades, M. (1998) *Understanding Children's Development* (3rd Edition), Blackwell. Ch. 14 – Again probably too much detail for A-level purposes but an additional source of information.

Smith, L., Dockrell, J. & Tomlinson, P.D. (Eds.) (1997) *Piaget, Vygotsky and Beyond*, Routledge. This book discusses the theories of Piaget and Vygotsky but also introduces new thinking on the topic of cognitive development.

4

The development of measured intelligence

Introduction

Intelligence is a very difficult thing to define. What is intelligence? What does it mean to be intelligent? These questions are very difficult to answer. Psychologists have produced many different definitions of intelligence, and even disagree about whether intelligence is one whole thing or a collection of different elements. For example, are you just an intelligent person or is intelligence made up of different aspects, like verbal skills, logic skills etc?

However, generally intelligence is seen to refer to 'differences in the ability to acquire information, to think and reason well and to deal effectively and adequately with the environment' (Cardwell, Clark, & Meldrum, 2000:460). Some aspects of intelligence can be measured and these aspects are tested by intelligence tests. It is important to note that these tests only measure certain aspects of intelligence. It could be said that they are addressing intellectual level not intelligence.

Therefore it is only possible to measure certain aspects of intelligence and it is the development of these measurable aspects that is the focus of this chapter.

There are a number of intelligence tests. These are standardised tests, in which the questions usually focus on logical reasoning and verbal and mathematical skills. They have clear instructions for administration and scoring. Each individual is therefore awarded a score after the test is marked. The tests allow comparison of performance either between groups or between individuals. There are some limitations of these tests, which will be discussed later.

Factors which affect measured intelligence

There is as much debate about which factors affect intelligence as there is about what intelligence actually is. The history of research into intelligence is extensive. Interest has focused on what causes the individual variations in intelligence levels. The most basic divide is between genetics (nature) and environmental factors (nurture). In other words, can the differences between individuals' intelligence levels be explained by genetic variations or by environmental variants? Non-genetic or environmental factors include all things that are not heritable. These factors are not just environmental stimulation and parenting, but also nutrition, illness, social economic status etc. The debate is therefore between the nativists, who suggest that knowledge and reasoning are genetically pre-structured, and the empiricists, who suggest that knowledge and reasoning come from experience and then mind is constructed and organised to reflect and make sense of these experiences (Richardson, 1999).

The question is even more complicated than this, as it is not clear *how much* of the differences in intelligence can be determined by nature (genetics) and how much by nurture (environment). As the intelligence debate has progressed still further, the psychometric approach to intelligence has tried to identify a general factor which is associated with intelligence. Recently research has begun to focus on the importance of genetics and the relationship between different aspects of intelligence, and has now moved to trying to identify genes associated with intelligence.

To try and investigate the influence of different aspects in the development of intelligence, a number of studies have been conducted.

This chapter will now discuss studies conducted into measured intelligence and review their findings, beginning by reviewing early research into the development of measured intelligence and progressing to a review of current research in this area.

Genetic factors in measured intelligence

Twin studies

Many of the studies designed to investigate the development of measured intelligence include twins. The reason for this is to try and compare individuals who share the same genetic make-up – this way researchers hope to be able to draw conclusions about which factors influence intelligence more, genetics or the environment. One way to compare individuals is by the use of IQ scores. To work out an individual's IQ score a test will be given to the individual, this test will measure factors such as mathematical reasoning, verbal abilities etc. Once a test is completed the individual's IQ score can be calculated, in general the higher the IQ score the more intelligent a person is thought to be. However, it is important to realise that there are some problems with IQ tests (see Intelligence tests and bias p. 75). The argument in terms of genetics and nature is investigating using IQ tests. If people are genetically the same but have different IQ scores, then this suggests that the environment is influential in determining intelligence.

Monozygotic (MZ) twins share the same genetic material as they come from the same egg and are therefore called 'identical twins'. Dizygotic (DZ) twins come from two separate eggs and therefore are like siblings genetically, the only difference being that they share the same pre-birth experience, unlike siblings who are in the womb separately.

Studies usually compare the IQ scores of the two twins and provide a correlation figure. A correlation of 1 is a perfect correlation and would mean that the scores are exactly the same. The further away from the figure of 1 a correlation is, the less meaningful it is. For example, a study that provided a correlation of 0.89 would show a high relationship between the two IQ scores, but one which resulted in a correlation of 0.2 shows a very low relationship and similarity between scores.

Shields (1962) conducted one of the earliest and most famous twin studies. Shields advertised for twins to take part in an experiment and obtained a sample of 44 twins. Some twins were brought up together, some apart. The twins' IQ levels were tested and compared. The MZ twins' correlation was 0.77 for those reared apart and 0.76 for those brought up together. This showed that the environment had little effect on intelligence because the correlations were almost identical. If the environment were an influential factor in the development of intelligence we would expect there to be a much greater difference between the correlations.

Evaluation

This study seemed to provide clear evidence that intelligence is determined by genetics but it has been heavily criticised, principally by Kamin (1977). He stated that Shields' sample was small. Also the claim that some of the twins in the study were brought up together and others apart was found to be questionable. There was not such a clear divide. When Kamin (1977) reviewed the study it was found that often twins said to have been reared apart actually spent large amounts of time together. Of the MZ twins, 14 were only reared apart after 1 year of age, and were often adopted by relatives and so continued to see each other. It is also known that adoption agencies try to match adoptive families with children. Part of this match is trying to place children in similar environments to make adaptation easier. Therefore it is not possible to say that the environments the twins were reared in were significantly different when they were reared apart. A third issue is that, like Piaget, Shields conducted experiments himself and like Piaget has been accused of experimenter bias. Also, a perfect correlation is 1.00, so what factors account for the difference between Shields' results and 1.00? It could be suggested that the difference is due to the environment and therefore environmental factors can be seen to be influential. The assumption that MZ twins are identical is also open to question. They are likely to have different birth experiences and also may be reared and related to differently by different parents. Thus their experience cannot be said to be completely identical and therefore they are not completely identical (Flanagan, 1997).

Other studies using twins have also been conducted. Kaufman (1999) and Bouchard and McGue (1981) conducted a review of a number of such studies. Pederson et al. (1992) reviewed the Swedish adoption / twin study of ageing, and Newman et al. (1928) also investigated IQ differences in MZ and DZ twins. The results of these studies are shown in Table 4.1. The table indicates what twin type the sample consisted of, what conditions they were brought up in – i.e. together or apart – and the correlation between their IQ scores when tested.

The results of these studies suggest that genetic factors are more influential on intelligence levels than environmental factors, as the twins that shared the same genetic material (MZ) had higher correlations than DZ twins however they had been brought up. This suggests that genetic factors are most important in determining intelligence levels. Pederson et al. (1992) suggested that about 80% of IQ is inherited. In a further study Bouchard et al. (1990) reviewed over 100 twins in a Minnesota study of twins reared apart. They found that about 70% of the IQ score is due to genetic factors. Kaufman (1999) suggests

Table 4.1 Summary of twin studies

Researchers	Twin type	Environment	Correlation of IQ score
Kaufman (1999)	MZ	Not specified	0.86
	DZ	Not specified	0.60
Bouchard & McGue (1981)	MZ	Not specified	0.85
	DZ	Not specified	0.58
Pederson et al. (1992)	MZ	Reared apart	0.79
		Reared together	0.79
	DZ	Reared apart	0.32
		Reared together	0.22
Newman et al. (1928)	MZ	Reared apart	0.67
		Reared together	0.91

that the heritability percentage for IQ is about 50%. Again this is compelling evidence for the influence of genetics.

However, if we revisit the criticisms made of Shields' study it can be seen that they could equally apply to these studies. They too could be accused of using small samples, claiming separation of twins when some contact remained, failing to recognise the adoption matching process, experimenter bias, failing to recognise that identical twins did not have identical experiences and failing to comment on the lack of a perfect correlation.

In a more recent twin study conducted in Australia it was found that at least 50% and perhaps 65% of the variation in educational achievements can be attributed to genetics. This study suggested that only 25% of the variation in educational achievement could be due to environmental factors (Miller, Mulvey, & Martin, 2001). This study provides support for the influence of genetics on intelligence and educational achievement.

Another large-scale twin study, which has been recently conducted, has given further support to the influence of genetics on the development of measured intelligence. In this study 209 sets of twins were tested at the ages of 5, 7, 10 and 12 years of age. The results of these IQ tests showed a significant influence of heritability at all ages and that the influence of genetics increased with age. The study suggested that genetic influences were the main causes of stability in cognitive abilities, again supporting the idea that intelligence may be largely genetically determined (Bartels, Rietveld, Van Baal, & Boomsma, D., 2002).

Alarcon, Knopik, and DeFries (2000) studied children's mathematic and general cognitive abilities. They found that 90% of the variability in maths performance and 80% of the variability in general cognitive performance were due to genetics.

De Geus, Wright, Martin, and Boomsma (2001) have provided a summary of research into the effects of genetic influences on individual differences and cognitive abilities, and have found overwhelming evidence for the existence of substantial genetic influences.

Familial studies

In addition to twin studies, familial or kinship studies have been conducted – these use as participants those who are blood relatives. Again

Table 4.2 Bouchard and McGue (1981) familial correlation study

Relationship	Environment	Correlation
MZ	RA	0.72
DZ	RT	0.60
MZ	RT	0.86
DZ	RT	0.60
Siblings	RT	0.47
Siblings	RA	0.24

RA – Reared apart; RT – Reared together

the reason is due to participants sharing some genetic information. Bouchard and McGue (1981) reviewed a large number of twin and familial studies to try to determine what factors were most influential in the development of intelligence. Their findings are shown in Table 4.2. This review study provided support for genetics – the closer the genetic link, the higher the correlation of IQ scores.

Evaluation

When considering the results it can be seen that there is still an imperfect correlation, so not all the IQ score can be determined by genetics. Also it is difficult to make a clear distinction between genetic influence and environmental influence. Siblings and twins reared together certainly share the same genetic information but also the same environment, to a large extent. Therefore it is difficult to determine if it is their shared environment that makes for a high correlation in IQ score. It is certainly presumptuous to assume it is the shared genetic information that influences the score.

Finally it is an advantage to group together a number of studies and review them, but in doing so you are grouping together different tests. Therefore it is difficult to ensure all the studies used are equal and this makes results questionable.

However, more recently a study was conducted by Segal, Weisfeld, G. & Weisfeld, C., (1997). She studied unrelated siblings of the same age reared together from infancy (this is the same as DZ twins). Her findings were an IQ correlation of only 0.17. This finding challenged the notion of shared experience making for a similar level of IQ and supported the theory that genetic information determined IQ. Segal suggested that individuals respond to environments based on their genetic predisposition. In other words, the environment interacts with genetics, but it is the genetics that mainly determine IQ.

Similarly, Kaufman (1999) also conducted a study and he found that correlations between a biological parent and a child living together (0.42) were higher than correlations between an adoptive parent and a child living together (0.19). Again this suggests the importance of genetic influence over environmental influence in determining IQ.

Finally Kaufman (1999) also compared the correlations of siblings, half siblings and cousins. Correlations for siblings were 0.47, as opposed to 0.31 for half siblings and 0.15 for cousins, again suggesting the importance of genetic influence.

Adoption studies

This chapter has reviewed twin and familial studies, and has discovered flaws with both methods of investigating measured intelligence. Another method used is to study children who have been adopted and compare their IQ scores with those of their birth or natural parents and their adoptive parents. The reasoning is that the children will share their genetic information with their natural parents and their environmental information or experience with their adoptive parents. Some of these studies will now be described and evaluated.

Horn (1983) conducted a study in Texas where a large adoption agency provided data which made this study possible. Unnamed mothers of 469 children who were adopted after birth were given IQ tests. The children were placed into 300 adoptive families. The IQs of the adoptive mothers were also measured. The IQ correlations were 0.15 for the adoptive mother and 0.28 for the natural mother. This shows some genetic influence on intelligence.

Plomin (1988) followed the children involved in the above study and reviewed their IQ scores at age 10. They had a correlation of just 0.02 with their adoptive siblings. Again this is evidence that a shared environment is not as influential as existing genetic information.

Stoolmiller (1998) raises questions over the design of the Texan adoption project and suggests that there was a 'gross underestimation of the effects of shared family environment'. However, this claim is disputed by Loehlin and Horn (2000).

Evaluation

This evidence suggests that there is usually a higher correlation between children and their natural parents than their adoptive parents, which is evidence for genetic influence. However, early in this chapter we reviewed the matching process that occurs in adoption. If environments are matched it is difficult to show that genetics are more influential in determining intelligence. Comparing adopted siblings can be seen to be flawed as it assumes that children's experiences within the same family are the same, i.e. the environment is constant. Studies of parenting suggest that siblings within the same family may have quite different experiences. Some factors which influence these experiences are: birth order, gender, temperament / personality and parental experience. Therefore being in the same family does not guarantee the same environment, which again puts some of the results and studies under question.

In addition, Kaufman (1999) suggests that the IQ of adopted parents and children living with them (0.19) is similar to that of biological parents and children living apart (0.22). This contradicts the findings of the Texan adoption project and does not suggest that genetic influences are much more influential than environmental ones. If this were the case, the second correlation should be much higher.

1. Why are twins used to study measured intelligence?

2. Outline the key details of one empirical study that suggests intelligence is genetically based.

Environmental factors

So far the evidence for and against genetic information determining intelligence has been reviewed. The evaluations of research have suggested that the environment may indeed be influential to some extent in determining intelligence. This section of the chapter will discuss a number of environmental factors and review the empirical studies conducted to determine the influence of these factors on measured intelligence.

Adoption studies

In the previous section we reviewed adoption studies primarily in investigating the role of genetics. Here we review them to investigate the role the environment plays. Scarr and Weinberg (1983) found that adopted children have IQ scores that are 10 to 20 points higher (on average) than their natural parents. This could be because adoptive families are generally better off financially and children in these environments can develop their full potential. Scarr and Weinberg (1977) also studied black children adopted by white families. As suggested previously these families had a higher financial and educational status than the natural family. The average IQ of the black adopted children was 106, and 110 when they were tested if they were adopted within 12 months of birth. This was compared with the average IQ of black children with similar genetic backgrounds but poorer environmental backgrounds. The IQ of these children was 90. Thus Scarr and Weinberg provided evidence for the role of the environment.

Schiff et al. (1978) found that children who were born to low social economic status parents but then adopted into high social economic status families showed significant IQ gains when compared to children left in the original environment.

Capron and Duyme (1989) studied 38 French children adopted in infancy. Half of these children had middle or upper class biological parents, half had working or lower class biological parents. Some of the infants were adopted into families that were from a higher social class than their biological parents, some into families from a lower social class. Children reared in upper class homes had IQ scores 15–16 points higher than those in lower class homes regardless of their biological parent class. This study emphasised the importance of the environment in the development of measured intelligence.

Evaluation

The earlier a child is adopted, the greater their intellectual improvement will be. This suggests that the environment is important and influential when it is provided in suitable circumstances. Age seems an important factor. The evidence suggests that the environment is most influential in pre-school years.

Studies involving children from different cultures are open to criticism. IQ tests have been criticised for being culturally biased (see later under test bias). They are thought to be based around white middle class values, ideas and experiences. Therefore improvements in black children's scores may not be actual intellectual improvements. They may not be any more intelligent, but because they are brought up in a white family the factors measured by the IQ test become more familiar and therefore they perform better. For example, I would fail a test paper written in a different language, but if it is translated I can pass. Similarly if a test uses unfamiliar objects and examples I fail – if I then come into contact with such objects and examples I am more likely to pass. I am not any more intelligent, I just understand the rules better.

Adoptive families are generally smaller and have a better financial and educational status. These factors make environmental influence seem stronger.

Although the study conducted by Capron and Duyme (1989) suggested the importance of the environment, genetic factors were also found to be important in this study. Children whose biological parents were from higher social economic status backgrounds had higher IQs than children whose biological parents were from lower social economic status backgrounds, regardless of the environment.

Familial studies

Kaufman (1999) provided evidence for the importance of the shared environment with reference to family studies. He found that the correlation for siblings reared together (0.47) was higher than for those reared apart (0.24). He also found that this was replicated by parents and children living together having a higher correlation of IQ scores (0.42) than for those living apart (0.22). This provides evidence for the importance of a shared environment and the influence of environment on the development of measured intelligence. If the environment were unimportant, the scores could be expected to be similar in both conditions.

Evaluation

The correlations are still quite low which suggests that other factors are also influential in the development of IQ.

Social economic status

Another factor that has been investigated is social economic status (SES). A number of studies have been conducted to see if there is any relationship between social economic status and intelligence levels.

Bernstein (1971) concentrated on the differences in language between low SES families and high SES families. He suggested from his research that children from low SES families had a restricted language code whereas children from high SES families had an elaborate language code. This means that in children from low SES families their language lacked abstract concepts, which made processing information difficult. This, Bernstein suggested, affected their cognitive development and verbal intelligence, and this argument supported the idea that intelligence can in fact be linked to social economic status.

A major longitudinal study, which followed children from birth to adolescence, was conducted by Sameroff et al. (1987). This was known as the Rochester Longitudinal Study and began in the 1970s.

It followed about 200 children. This study identified 10 factors that could affect IQ score. These factors were not genetic but environmental. They were:

- Parental mental illness
- Serious parental anxiety
- Father living away from family
- Child is a minority group member
- Four or more children in family
- Many parental stressful life events in child's pre-school years
- Lack of maternal interaction and positive attention
- Rigid parental beliefs about child's development
- Lack of secondary education in parents
- Poor parental employment

The more of these factors a child encountered, the lower their IQ score was. Each factor seemed to reduce IQ by about 4 points.

Evaluation

Labov (1970) criticised Bernstein's study by stating that he confused linguistic and social deprivation. That is, that poor language skills are not the same as a poor social environment. Also Labov claimed that Bernstein had failed to take account of the studies on non-standard English. Some children used the English language differently from others and this was not taken into account.

Although Sameroff's study seems to provide evidence that IQ intelligence level is linked to social economic status, it is actually showing that factors associated with belonging to a lower social economic status group, and not social economic status itself, affect IQ.

Another factor to consider is that individuals in lower social economic status groups may be genetically less intelligent which is why they do not achieve educationally and therefore obtain unskilled / semi-skilled employment and become part of the lower classes. This, then, is an argument for genetics not environment. If intelligence is genetically determined, it is logical that individuals with lower IQs will have lower social economic status (Flanagan, 1997).

Other factors which are not genetic can be related to parenting. Parents have a great influence over the environment in which their children develop. The following sections will discuss a number of other environmental factors that may affect intelligence.

Diet

Benton and Cook (1991) provided one group of children with vitamin supplements and a control group were given placebos. When the children's IQs were tested, the children who had received supplements had increased their IQ score by 7.6 points and the placebo group decreased by 1.7 points. This was a double blind study and therefore the children did not know what was expected. The results are quite compelling.

Daley, Whaley, Sigman, Epinosa and Neumann (2003) note that many studies have shown that IQ levels have increased over time – this increase is known as the **Flynn effect**. They state that results from 20 industrialised nations have shown large IQ gains over time. They suggest that among the reasons for this increase is better nutrition in children. This research may help to explain why children from low SES groups have lower IQ, as their diets are often poorer and this may affect their IQ.

Berkman, Lescano, Gilman, Lopez and Black (2002) investi-gated the effect of chronic malnutrition on cognitive ability. They tested children at age 9 and found that those who had a poor diet and stunted growth at age 2 scored 10 points lower on cognitive tests at age 9 than their peers who were not malnourished. Black suggested that this study emphasises the importance of nutrition to children under 3, again providing evidence for a link between diet and cognitive ability.

Research conducted into children living in shanty housing in India showed that malnutrition before the age of 6 months had a significant influence on IQ (Choudhary, Sharma, Agarwal, Kumar, Sreenivas, & Puliyel, 2002). Again this suggests a link between early diet and intelligence.

Benton (2001) comments on a review of studies investigating the link between nutritional supplements and intelligence levels in children. In 10 out of 13 studies there was a positive response to these supplements in at least part of the experimental sample. The evidence suggests that not all children respond to supplements but a minority of children do, and this has an effect particularly on their non-verbal abilities. However, it seems that children who do respond have diets that consist of low levels of nutrients. It may be that the results show normal levels of functioning on a normal diet.

One problem with investigating diet is that it is difficult to fully monitor an individual's diet and therefore to be completely sure of food intake. This makes conclusions about the link between diet and intelligence open to question. Another problem is that to illustrate the effect of diet other factors need to be constant, to show that diet is making a difference. It is difficult to monitor all environmental factors and again therefore difficult to show that diet is a determining factor. This argument can be seen if we return to the early study of Indian children living in a shanty town. Although early diet was identified as influential in determining IQ, so were pre-school education and housing. Children in permanent housing had higher IQs and were more likely to attend pre-school. Similarly the study conducted into the Flynn effect also identified parents' literacy and family structure as factors influencing the increase in IQ levels. It can be difficult to establish the link between environmental factors and IQ.

Parental stimulation

Hart and Risley (1995) conducted a long-term developmental investigation. They focused on verbal interactions. They found that all children started to talk at the same age but there were differences at the age of 3. Children from professional families had a much broader vocabulary than working class children. Hart and Risley related this to parental behaviour. They suggested a relationship between parental stimulation and language development.

Caldwell and Bradley (1978) found a correlation between high IQ scores and the following factors: emotionally responsive parenting, provision of appropriate play materials, opportunities to play and learn, parents' expectations. Good IQ scores were related to parents who expected children to achieve and to learn. Caldwell and Bradley developed a scale called the Home Observation for Measurement of the Environment (HOME). They found low scores on the HOME scale in infancy correlated to low IQ scores at school.

Crandell and Hobson (1999) found evidence for a link between attachment and IQ. A sample of 36 mothers were divided into two groups based on their response to an attachment interview and questionnaire. The mothers were given an IQ test and the children were given an abbreviated version. The mother–child interactions were assessed by video tape. Children of secure mothers scored 19 points higher on the test. A sub-group of 12 secure and 12 insecure mothers were matched by IQ score, and there was still a significant difference between the children's IQ scores. This suggests that attachment was more of an influential factor than parental IQ. This study emphasised the importance of attachment and the child's social environment in the development of measured intelligence.

Sigman et al. (1988) found that parents of higher IQ children talk to them often in a rich, detailed and accurate manner, once more illustrating the importance of parental stimulation. Laundry et al. (1996) found that parents of higher IQ children work in the ZPD (see Chapter 3) – they talk to their children just above their current level of understanding and use strategies to help them learn new skills. Pianta and Egeland (1994) found that parents of higher IQ children provided them with age-appropriate toys and play.

A project entitled the Abecedanan Project followed infants from poor-level families whose mothers had low IQ scores. The children were assigned to one of two groups – a control or experimental group. In the control group, children were given nutritional supplements and medical care. In the experimental group, children were given both of these factors but also enriched day care. This began at 6–12 weeks and continued until the children began kindergarten. The IQ scores were higher for the experimental group at every test between 2 and 12 years – 44% of the control group had borderline IQ scores in comparison to only 12.8% of the experimental group (Ramey & Campbell, 1987; Ramey, 1993).

This study again seemed to show how important a rich environment is in developing measured intelligence. Indeed the richness of the environment was more influential than the supplements and medical care.

Again it must be recognised that children may receive more stimulation and educational encouragement as a consequence of their parent's high IQ. Thus a parent possessing a high IQ may put more emphasis on education and stimulation. Therefore this is not automatically an argument for the environment – the environment may be created because of a genetically determined high IQ.

It is important to recognise finance as a factor. Parents with higher IQs are likely to have better jobs and therefore more disposable income. This allows for the purchase of appropriate toys and learning materials and extra educational support.

It should be noted that attachment is a highly controversial subject. In Crandell and Hobson's study the assumption is made that the difference in IQ levels is simply due to difference in attachment. However, problems with attachment may indicate problems in other areas of the social and emotional environment of the child, which may be masked by the focus on attachment.

Plomin and Petrill (1997) suggest that half of the HOME prediction of differences in cognitive abilities of children can be accounted for by genetic and not environmental factors.

Birth order

Zajonc and Markus (1975) investigated birth order and IQ, and reviewed IQ scores of 40,000 Dutch males. They found that the IQ scores declined with family size and birth order. This could be because as each child is born parents have to share their attention and time more, and often finances become stretched.

Zajonc (2001) developed a model called the confluence model. This model states that the intelligence of each family member depends on other family members. He suggests that each successive child comes into a weaker intellectual environment and that the intellectual environment improves with decreasing family size. Part of the reason that firstborns tend to have higher IQs is that they act as tutors to their siblings, and therefore teach them and explain things to them thereby increasing their own understanding and IQ. By contrast younger children do not have to explain ideas, and others always have a ready answer – younger children do not therefore have to develop their thinking and reasoning skills so much.

Evaluation

The relationship between birth order and intelligence has been greatly debated. Lowery (1995) tested students' intelligence levels and collected information about birth order. She found no significant relationship between birth order and intelligence, and concluded that birth order does not have an effect on intelligence. Rodgers, Cleveland, Van den Oord and Rowe (2001) claim that the link between birth order and intelligence is an illusion, and in their studies found no consistent relationship between these factors.

Recent developments in the study of intelligence

The psychometric approach to intelligence

The arguments for and against the importance of genetic and environmental factors in the development of measured intelligence have been reviewed. However, as stated in the introduction, the debate about the origin of individual differences in intelligence levels has entered new areas and has moved to focus on new and important questions.

Kline (1991) is a supporter of the psychometric approach to intelligence. This approach attempts to identify correlations between different aspects of intelligence. This approach would suggest that individuals who are viewed as intelligent would score highly on different measures of intelligence. Therefore they can be seen to have a general intelligence factor. The psychometric approach suggests that this general factor can be known as 'g' and that 'g' is common to all problem-solving abilities. The psychometric approach suggests that 'g' is combined with specific abilities in a particular area to make an individual intelligent in that area. For example an accomplished musician would have 'g' + music factor, a gifted mathematician would have 'g'+ maths factor. So Kline is suggesting that there is a general factor of intelligence, which is fundamental to problem solving in any area, and that this is combined with specific abilities. 'g' is made up of two types of intelligence – fluid intelligence and crystallised intelligence. Fluid intelligence is the basic reasoning ability. Crystallised intelligence is this ability shown through skills valued by the culture in which the individual lives. So, an individual may have a basic ability in maths, but this is shown and recognised when they become an accountant.

The psychometric approach suggests that 70% of intelligence differences are due to biological factors and 30% due to environmental factors (Sternberg & Wagner, 1986). This approach moves away from the basic nature–nurture debate and provides an explanation for intelligence. However, it has been criticised for not explaining what 'g' actually is and how it works (Sternberg, 1986). Also, as will now be discussed, intelligence develops across the lifespan and does not simply mature, and this is difficult for the psychometric approach to explain.

Plomin's contribution

Plomin and Petrill (1997) suggest that the intelligence debate has moved away from the basic nature–nurture issue. There has been a general assumption that if intelligence is genetically based it must be fixed and cannot be changed. Thus if you are born intelligent, you stay intelligent, and if not, you stay unintelligent. Plomin and Petrill argue that even if there is a genetic basis to intelligence this could still be influenced by new environmental experiences. They recognise that 75 years of research with twins, familial studies and adoption studies have provided strong evidence for the influence of genetics. However, they estimate the influence of heritability at 50% not 80% as has been suggested. Interestingly and importantly, Plomin and Petrill have found that the influence of heritability is not a static factor. The assumption has been that you could identify the influence of heritability and that this was a set influence. However, research has shown that heritability increases from 20% in infancy to 40% in early childhood to 60% in early adulthood to 80% in later life (Plomin, 1997). A Swedish study of twins reared apart and together provided support for the increasing heritability. The study yielded an 80% heritability estimate at 60 years of age, and this was replicated three years later (Pederson et al., 1992). Thus heritability is not constant and it becomes more important as life progresses.

However, Plomin and Petrill recognise that there are some problems with studying heritability. Most studies have been conducted in the USA and Europe, and therefore the results may be culturally biased. Also research has focused upon the normal range of intelligence and there is little research into high and low levels of intelligence, which may provide essential information for understanding of the development of measured intelligence. Finally most studies are conducted on children and, as Plomin's recent research suggests, it is important to study adults or conduct longitudinal studies to fully investigate heritability. In addition to these factors there are general criticisms of IQ tests (see earlier).

Moving on in the study of intelligence, Plomin uses genetic research to suggest that there is a link between different abilities, and that some abilities are more heritable than others. For example, spatial and verbal abilities seem to be more heritable than memory abilities. In addition, researchers have begun to use what is known as multivariate genetic analysis to investigate the relationship between different abilities. Put simply, it appears that some abilities are more strongly related to others, and have a strong degree of genetic influence and overlap, so if you have excellent verbal abilities you are likely to also have good spatial abilities (Plomin & DeFries, 1979).

However, although Plomin seems to concentrate on the influence of genetics and heritability, he is also interested in the environment. If 50% of the difference in IQ scores can be explained by heritability, this must mean that the other 50% is not genetically based. Plomin suggests that it is as important to concentrate on non-shared environmental experiences as on shared experiences. He suggests that shared environmental factors account for about 30% of IQ differences. However, Plomin comments on a study conducted by Loehlin, Horn and Willerman (1989) which was a 10-year follow-up study of 181 adopted siblings. The study showed that the correlation between their IQ scores was 0.26 at 8 years of age, but at 18 it was –0.1. This suggested that shared family environments might have an early effect on IQ, but that this effect diminishes in adolescence. This confirms Plomin's early suggestions that heritability becomes more important across the lifespan.

Plomin suggests that research into family environments needs to be clearly designed to separate the influence of genetics and environment. Also he suggests that children actively choose and develop their environments, and that there is an active interaction between genetics and the environment. Therefore genes can actually influence and contribute to the experience of the environment. We often think that it is the environment that impacts the individual, but Plomin suggests that genes can interact with the environment, making differences in experiences, learning and the development of intelligence.

The latest development in the debate over intelligence is genetic research, which is seeking to identify specific genes that are responsible for the influence of genetics on intelligence. Research is trying to identify genes which can be shown as contributing to intelligence. The intention is not to identify a single gene – the thinking is that there are many genes, which contribute to the differences in intelligence levels between individuals. Research has tended to focus upon genes associated with disorders – e.g. Fragile X syndrome – but this research has found links between a specific gene and this disorder, suggesting a genetic basis to parts of intelligence. Research has also identified genes associated with low intelligence (Wahlsten, 1990).

The implications of such research would be that children might differ in their ability to learn, at least in part, for genetic reasons. This would have real educational implications and it is difficult to see how it could be responded to. Also it may be the case that more intelligent children are genetically programmed to learn more quickly and to learn more. However, the interaction between genetics and the environment should not be forgotten.

This section has illustrated the latest developments in the intelligence debate. It is important to recognise that IQ tests are used as the basis for many research studies in this area. If IQ tests are flawed, then the research produced using them is also open to question. The next section will review issues surrounding IQ tests.

Intelligence tests and bias

Obviously the tests used to measure intelligence are very important. Decisions about jobs and educational placement are made on the basis of these test results. If these tests are flawed, then the results are also open to question, therefore subsequent decisions based on these results are also questionable. Judgements about the nature–nurture debate are also based on these tests. Therefore if the tests are flawed the whole debate may also be open to question. If we refer back to the earlier twin studies, we can see that the results are presented as correlations of IQ test scores. On the basis of these results researchers make a decision about whether genetics or the environment is more influential in determining the development of intelligence. However, if the IQ tests are unreliable, so are any conclusions drawn from them. Richardson (2002) suggests that IQ tests are a measure of social economic status and not intelligence.

Cultural bias

Intelligence tests appear to be written for particular cultures and therefore individuals from other cultures may well perform badly at them even though they may actually be very intelligent. Code, Gay, Glick and Sharp (1971) studied Nigerians completing a classification task, which they consistently failed until they were asked to sort it as a stupid person would. Then they used European categories and passed the test!

Earlier we reviewed Scarr and Weinberg's (1983) study of black adopted children that illustrated an improvement in their IQ scores when adopted by white families. Obviously, if IQ tests are written for a white middle class culture, then as children spend time in this environment they pick up values and skills accordingly and therefore increase their performance. This does not indicate any *real* improvement in intelligence. Heath (1989) studied black children and their mothers and found that black mothers asked questions that required long answers, which helped their children's general education but did not prepare them for the short answers needed on the IQ tests. This suggests cultural bias.

Craig and Beishuizen (2002) suggest that IQ tests may be culturally biased and what they might actually be testing is the effectiveness of intercultural education – that is, how effectively minority group members have been socialised into the Western culture and can therefore answer questions presented in a culturally biased way.

Motivation and anxiety

Zigler et al. (1973) found that lower SES children improved their test performance if they were allowed to play with the tester before the test began. There was less effect with middle SES children.

Teacher expectation is also a factor. In a study by Rosenthal and Jacobsen (1968), teachers were informed that individual children were expected to make great progress. This information directly affected the way in which the teachers interacted with these children. Thus the information became a self-fulfilling prophecy. The teachers' behaviour impacted the children's performance, and those children who had been identified at the beginning were seen to make the most progress. The progress the children made was not based on their intelligence levels at the beginning of the research, but appeared to be based on the teachers' expectations and subsequent behaviour towards them. Children identified had very large IQ gains, suggesting a self-fulfilling prophecy. We will do well if we are expected to, and we know this.

Evaluation of IQ tests

All these factors suggest that IQ test results can be open to question and that IQ level is not necessarily set. This has led researchers to question whether intelligence can really be tested in this way, and whether intelligence is not about certain testable qualities but is better thought of as the ability to adapt to situation. Garlick (2002) suggests that those with low IQ perform poorly because they cannot adapt well to the environmental situation. Those who seem intelligent are those who can adapt themselves and their knowledge to different situations.

Summary

Intelligence tests have been designed to measure different aspects of intelligence. The fundamental question is whether intelligence is determined by nature or nurture. In order to investigate the effects of genetics, researchers have used twin, familial and adoption studies. Researchers have also identified environmental factors which can influence the development of measured intelligence. These include social class, diet, parental stimulation and birth order. IQ tests are used to measure intelligence, but they have been criticised on the grounds that they are culturally biased and that test results can be affected by motivation and anxiety. Children's results could be inflated or depressed by elements of the tests themselves.

There is still much debate about what intelligence is and how it should be measured. There is no clear answer to the question of how much of a child's intelligence is determined by nature and how much by nurture. Studies have provided evidence for factors that seem to be influential in determining intelligence levels. However, tests used to measure intelligence have been criticised. This has led to renewed questions about the nature of intelligence. Research and debates into the development of measured intelligence are set to continue.

Further reading

Plomin, R. & Petrill, S.A. (1997) Genetics and intelligence: What's new? *Intelligence*, *24*(1), pp. 53–77.

The development of moral understanding

In earlier chapters, theories of cognitive development and the development of measured intelligence were reviewed. In addition to the development of measured intelligence, another aspect of cognitive development is the development of moral understanding. In the same way that children try to make sense of the world generally, they also try to decide what is right and what is wrong, this is known as **moral judgement**. Children also have to decide how to behave in a moral situation, this is known as **moral behaviour**. Moral judgement develops and changes as the child grows. There is a link with general cognitive development in that certain moral judgements require complicated thinking. It is generally expected that children will develop their morality, and that this development is dependent on their general cognitive development and maturation processes. In this chapter, two of the main theories in this area, those of Piaget and Kohlberg, will be reviewed. Then an evaluation of these theories will be presented and then the discussion of moral development will continue making reference to Eisenberg's theory of pro-social reasoning. To conclude, a discussion of the relationship between gender and moral development, and culture and moral development, will be presented.

Piaget

Earlier in this book Piaget's stage model of cognitive development was discussed (see Chapter 2). Piaget was fascinated by the way in which children's understanding of the world develops. It is not surprising that this interest combined with Piaget's philosophical background resulted in an interest in moral development.

Through his observation of children and his experiments Piaget developed a stage theory of moral development. This was similar to his theory of cognitive development in that each stage built upon the previous stage. Each stage represents a qualitatively different stage of moral development. He used two main tools to investigate the development of morality. He observed children playing marbles and monitored their beliefs about the rules of marbles. He also told **moral stories** or **vignettes** in which he asked children to make a moral judgement about another child's actions. These stories contrasted the behaviour and actions of two different children. Piaget was interested to see how children made judgements about what is right and wrong behaviour, and what the basis of these judgements was. An example of one of these pairs of moral stories can be seen in Table 5.1.

Piaget told children the pairs of stories and then asked questions about these stories, such as those listed in Table 5.1. These included asking who was the naughtiest and why. By recording children's responses to such stories and their playing of marbles, Piaget was able to observe a progression and development in children's morality – again this development was linked to specific ages. The changes in reasoning and ideas about what is morally right and wrong can be seen in the example in Table 5.1.

Piaget's stage model of moral development

Based on his research with children and his observation of their responses to the moral dilemmas and their playing of the game of

Table 5.1 Piaget's moral stories

Story A Alfred meets a little friend of his who is very poor. This friend tells him that he has had no dinner that day because there was nothing to eat in his home. Then Alfred goes into a baker's shop, and as he has no money, he waits till the baker's back is turned and steals a roll. The he runs out and gives the roll to his friend.

Story B Henriette goes into a shop. She sees a pretty piece of ribbon on a table and thinks to herself that it would look very nice on her dress. So while the shop lady's back is turned (while the shop lady is not looking) she steals the ribbon and runs away at once.

Children's responses during interview
Child 1 "SCHMA" 6 year old
Is of these children naughtier than the other? *The boy is, because he took a roll. It's bigger.*
Ought they to be punished? *Yes. Four slaps for the first.*
And the girl? *Two slaps.*
Why he did take the roll? *Because his friend had had no dinner.*
And the other child? *To make herself pretty.*

Child 2 "Geo" 6 year old
Which of them is naughtiest? *The one with the roll because the roll is bigger than the ribbon*

Child 3 "Corm" 9 year old
What do you think about it? *Well, the little boy oughtn't to have stolen. He oughtn't to have stolen it but to have paid for it. And the other one, she oughtn't to have stolen the ribbon either.*
Which of them is the naughtiest? *The little girl took the ribbon for herself. The little boy took the roll too, but to give to his friend who had no dinner.*
If you were the school teacher, which one would you punish most? *The little girl.* (pp.127–128)

The stories of the roll and the ribbon (p.119) from *The Moral Judgement of the Child* (1932).

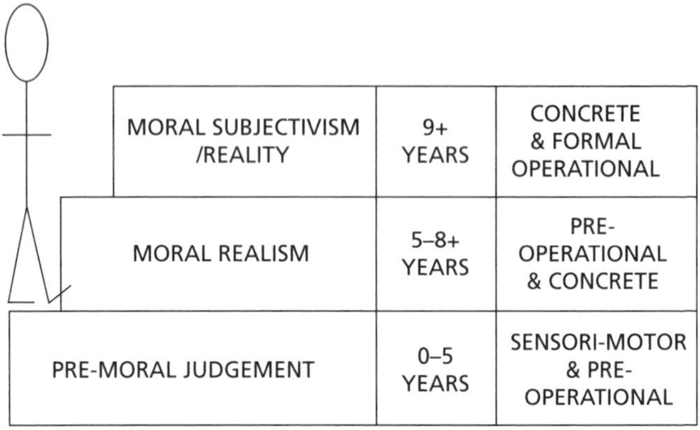

MORAL SUBJECTIVISM /REALITY	9+ YEARS	CONCRETE & FORMAL OPERATIONAL
MORAL REALISM	5–8+ YEARS	PRE-OPERATIONAL & CONCRETE
PRE-MORAL JUDGEMENT	0–5 YEARS	SENSORI-MOTOR & PRE-OPERATIONAL

Figure 5.1 Piaget's stage model of moral development

marbles, Piaget noted that children's moral understanding and reasoning changed as they developed. On the basis of his research he constructed the stage model seen in Figure 5.1. In Table 5.2 the major characteristics of each stage of Piaget's model are described and the differences between the stages are clearly identified.

Piaget linked the development of moral reasoning with cognitive changes. He thought that the decline in egocentrism and growth in operational thought was extremely relevant to children's more developed moral understanding. To develop a sense of moral understanding you need to be able to view problems from different perspectives and not to simply see the world from your point of view. For example, taking toys from other children is a common activity for toddlers. Most adults and indeed older children would view taking toys from someone else as wrong. However to an egocentric child it makes sense if you see the world from your viewpoint – the toy will make you happy, you don't understand rules or the perspective of others, so to you, it is the right choice.

Therefore Piaget saw moral development to be intertwined with and dependent on cognitive development. Piaget also noted the importance of interaction with peers in the development of moral understanding. He felt this was important, to allow the child to begin to understand the different perspectives other people have and to learn to resolve conflicts that arise, for example, who has the toy that everyone wants.

Table 5.2 A description of Piaget's stage model of moral development

Pre-moral judgement 0–5	Moral realism	Moral relativism
This stage is characterised by an inability to understand rules. A child will find it difficult to stick to the rule of no sweets before tea as they do not understand the rationale for the rule.	**Moral absolutes** – At this stage rules are sacred and fixed and cannot be changed. Morals at this stage are controlled by others, usually parents. (This is known as **heteronomous morals**.)	Morals are self-determined (**autonomous morals**). During this stage children develop their own sense and set of morals .
	Judge behaviour on consequences of actions not intention. In the example of the 'roll and the ribbon' moral stories in Table 5.1 the younger children made the judgement that the boy was naughtiest because the roll was bigger. They did not make a judgement on the intentions of the children, just the consequences of their actions.	Intention is the most important factor in judging behaviour not consequences. If we return to the example of the moral story in Table 5.1 we can see that the older child judged the girl to be more naughty as she was stealing for herself and the boy was stealing to help someone else. The judgement here is not on the consequence as much as the intention behind the behaviour.

continued . . .

Table 5.2 continued

Pre-moral judgement 0–5	Moral realism	Moral relativism
Inability to understand rule violation. The child does not understand that it is wrong to take toys from other children at this stage, and this is a reflection of their egocentric thought.	Punishment by someone who is in a position of authority is accepted. **Collective punishment** is seen to be fair. This is where a group of children are all punished because the person in authority does not know who was at fault. For example a class of children at nursery school may all be stopped from going out to play as one of them poured paint over the floor but the teachers do not know who did this.	Collective punishment is judged as unfair. That is, punishing everyone if you don't know who did something. Punishments given should fit the crime (**reciprocity**). The punishment should be equivalent to the wrongness of the behaviour. Stealing a biscuit from the tin receives less punishment than deliberately hitting someone.
	Children see rules as real things (**realism**).	Rules can be changed by mutual consent (**relativism**).

By interaction children learn to develop ways of dealing with conflict and that they can create rules, and therefore that rules are not static – an important stage of moral development.

A modern example concerning the moral development of children, which is extremely relevant, is that of the killing of the toddler Jamie Bulger. There has been much debate about whether the two boys who killed him were morally responsible for their actions. Some individuals feel that they were too young to understand the consequences of their actions; others believe that at the age of 10 moral development has occurred to such an extent that they would have been fully aware of their actions.

What does Piaget's theory suggest and how would he have explained their actions? The boys responsible were 10 at the time that they killed the toddler. Therefore they were at the moral relativism stage. At this stage, Piaget suggested, children can form their own morals. This may explain why the boys behaved in a way considered unacceptable to others. If they had constructed their own morals, hurting another child may have become morally acceptable to them. Piaget also emphasises the importance of peers in the development of morals, and through discussion new moral values can be constructed, and in this case two peers were involved. Interestingly, though, at this stage intentions are seen to be more important than consequences, so Piaget may well have asked what was the intention of the boys, rather than concentrating on the consequences. Also, in deciding whether they were morally responsible it may be more appropriate to concentrate on their initial intentions rather than the consequences of their actions. We cannot make a judgement because we do not know their initial intentions.

As Piaget's theory suggests that at this stage reciprocity is the key to punishment, the boys would have expected a severe sentence to match the severity of the crime. However, Piaget may argue that they should be judged more on their intentions than the consequences, and also that as these children were at the concrete operational stage of development (see Chapter 2) they did not have the cognitive ability to logically deduce the consequences of their actions. They may not have been able to fully understand the consequences for Jamie or themselves.

Piaget's theory cannot provide a full answer to the questions that have been raised by the Jamie Bulger case but it can allow us to explore, from Piaget's viewpoint, the moral stage the young killers may have reached.

Some of the empirical evidence in support of and in opposition to Piaget's theory of moral development will now be discussed.

Evaluation of Piaget's theory

In support of Piaget

Piaget (1932) played marbles with children, he observed them and questioned them about rules and their use of them. Children under 3 played without any rules. By age 5, rules were seen as absolute and set by an unknown authority. By age 10 the children realised that other individuals had set the original rules and that they could be changed. Linaza (1984) studied Spanish children and found the same stages of development and the same sequence, supporting Piaget's theory.

Piaget (1932) used moral stories to study how children make moral judgements and whether they make judgements on the basis of consequences or intentions. As discussed earlier, Piaget used pairs of stories. In one story the consequences were bigger but the intentions were good. In the second the consequences were smaller but the intentions were wrong. Younger children made judgements based on the consequences not the intentions. Older children made judgements based on the intentions not the consequences.

Narvaes (2001) reviewed a number of studies of moral text comprehension, where children were studied to see how they understood moral stories. Narvaes found significant differences in understanding of moral stories based on age and level of expertise. He also found that younger children do not understand moral themes. This supports Piaget's links between moral development and cognitive development, and suggests that age is a factor in the development of moral understanding. Also Narvaes' findings suggest different levels of moral understanding. Further, Narvaes suggests an absence of moral understanding in young children, as they were unable to understand moral themes, supporting Piaget's pre-moral stage.

Youniss and Volpe (1978) supported Piaget's idea of the importance of authority figures in young children's development of morals. In their study they found that parents, who were authority figures, acted as a source of moral knowledge for heteronomous reasoners. Peers, however, were used by autonomous reasoners to discuss ideas with and possibly construct new moral ideas. This supports Piaget's notion of heteronomous and autonomous reasoners, and also the importance of the authority figure in young children's learning of morals.

Smetana (1999) investigated the role of parents in moral development, and found that parents who were sensitive to the developmental stage of their child and provided reasoning that matched their child's stage of development promoted moral development. This suggests that moral reasoning does develop and is different at different ages. This research supports the notion of different stages of reasoning as Piaget stated.

Peterson and Siegal (2002) investigated the relationship between friendship and moral development. They studied 109 children, with an average age of 4.8 years, who were divided into groups based on measures of friendships. They were divided into popular and rejected pre-schoolers. Rejected children who had a stable mutual friend scored higher on measures of moral understanding and theory than did rejected children without such a friendship. There was no difference in measures of moral understanding between popular children related to a stable mutual friendship. Peterson and Siegal found that peer popularity was a significant predicator of children's moral understanding. Children without friendships and who lack frequent interaction obtain a lower score on measure of moral understanding. This study supports Piaget's emphasis on the importance of peer interaction in the development of moral understanding.

In opposition to Piaget

Nelson (1980) found that if children were provided with clear explicit information and detailed explanations of moral stories, then children as young as 3 could make judgements about intentions.

Ferguson and Rule (1982) provided an example of a child pushing another child off some wall bars. Young children judged that the intention to hurt another child severely was worse than the intention to hurt a little. Older children felt that the intention to hurt was wrong whatever the severity of intent. This illustrated a degree of support for Piaget as the children's morals were seen to develop, but in contrast to Piaget's ideas the experiment illustrated that young children do judge by intention.

Chandler et al. (1973) used the moral stories method but showed videotaped versions rather than telling the story verbally. Using this method they found that 6 year olds were just as capable of recognising intention as older children.

Smetana (1981) studied American children aged 2–5 and found that they were able to judge behaviour and rule breaking, and to make distinctions between rules and distinctions between punishments. This suggests that, as in his study of cognitive development, Piaget under-estimated children's development of moral reasoning.

Laupa (1991) conducted a study to investigate the idea that young children base their moral judgements on those made by people in authority over them, and that these judgements are absolute and cannot be argued with. The children were asked if an action that is usually considered morally wrong – e.g. hitting another child – would be right if an adult condoned it. The assumption would be that if authority judgements are always right, the children would think that if an adult said it was all right then it was. However, young children's responses indicated that they thought it was *wrong* even if an adult in authority said it was right. This contradicts Piaget's idea that young children see authority's decisions as absolute.

Evaluation of Piaget's methods of investigation

Kamii (1978) criticised the use and presentation of the moral dilemma stories. As the consequences were often large (breaking 15 cups in one story!) children are actively encouraged to concentrate on the conse-quences. Kamii also thought that often the bad or wrong intention was not definite but inferred. For example the boy who was looking for jam when he broke a cup may not have been being naughty – children are not told that he shouldn't have been looking in the cupboard. Therefore this is quite a difficult intention to judge.

Kail (1990) discussed the problem of memory. The verbal stories require good memory skills, this may be why children make judge-ments on consequences, as these are the last things they are told and therefore the easiest to recall.

Turiel (1983) pointed out that the game of marbles is not the most effective or valid method to test moral behaviour. Piaget did not take into account the process of socialisation or the importance of the influence of others in the child's moral development. Smetana (1999) did lend support to Piaget's notion of development but also illustrated the significant effect that parents who were sensitive to their child's development, provided developmentally sensitive reasoning and expla-nations stimulated the development of more mature moral thought.

Evaluation of Piaget's contribution

Piaget developed a stage model of moral development which linked stages of moral development to cognitive maturity – thinking changes as a consequence of biological maturation which affects the way a child thinks and moral understanding is a kind of thinking. However, his work has been subject to various criticisms.

Inappropriate methods of investigation

Piaget's methods were criticised as being inappropriate (games of marbles) and complex (moral stories). As with his earlier experiments, Piaget did not conduct clearly controlled experiments and again was accused of experimenter bias. He provided children with pretend or theoretical situations – how children answer in these situations may not indicate how they actually behave in real situations.

Underestimation of children's abilities

Piaget was seen in Chapter 2 to underestimate children's cognitive abilities; he is also accused of underestimating children's moral development and the complexity of moral development. Subsequent studies discussed in this chapter have illustrated that children can reach stages of moral development earlier than Piaget stated. Young children have been seen to question authority moral decisions and to make judgements on the basis of consequences.

Inconsistency between moral judgements and moral behaviour

Piaget did not include a discussion of inconsistency – that is, that children might make a decision in response to the moral stories, or they might provide an answer of how they would behave, but their actual moral behaviour does not match their moral judgements. Piaget did not investigate whether the children's moral behaviour was consistent with their moral judgements.

Gender

Piaget's work has been criticised for being gender specific. Weinreich-Haste (1982) criticises Piaget's theory for being based around rules and rationality, and states that this is more relevant to a 'male' notion of morality (see later discussion of Gilligan's work).

Social and cultural factors

Piaget's work has also been criticised for ignoring the importance of social and cultural factors in the development of morals. Smetana (1999) argues for the importance of parents in encouraging children's moral development and thinking. This research suggests that parents can promote moral development by offering explanations and reasons for moral decisions to children. These explanations need to be matched to the child's developmental level in order that they can understand them. Smenta's work would suggest that children can be encouraged to develop their moral understanding by interaction with parents, and so social interaction is an important part of moral development. Therefore moral understanding is not necessarily age-related and could well depend on socialisation, i.e. the influence of others.

Buck-Morss (1975) suggests that Piaget's emphasis on the developmental process makes his work open to the criticism that he has ignored the important impact that social and cultural differences can have on moral development. In Northern Ireland there is a moral disagreement with abortion. Children developing there are likely to be surrounded with arguments against abortion and be provided with the reasons why this is morally wrong. These arguments may be provided by schools and parents and reinforced in general policy. In England abortion is not such an important cultural issue and therefore children developing there are likely to hear both sides of the debate. Children developing in different countries will be exposed to different moral ideas and the influence of culture should not be ignored. (See later discussion on culture.)

Moral development and cognitive development

Piaget's work did suggest a link between moral development and cognitive development and this link has been supported by his own research and that of the studies in the section entitled In support of Piaget.

Children's development of moral understanding

Although Piaget may have underestimated the ages at which children reach the different stages, his work was influential in that, as with cognitive development, Piaget noted that children's moral thinking develops, and that it *is* different from adult thinking. Even research which has been used to dispute some of the claims of Piaget has provided evidence to support some of his ideas. For example in Laupa's (1991) study which illustrated children disagreeing with authority figures, her results also indicated that young children did show some features of heteronomy. Also in Smetana's (1999) study children were seen to need different explanations of moral decisions depending on their level of development, suggesting different levels of moral understanding.

Piaget saw interaction with peers as an essential part of moral development. Kruger (1992) investigated the role of peers in the development of moral understanding. He paired 8-year-old children with a peer or an adult. The pairs were asked to discuss moral dilemmas. In the discussion about the dilemma those children paired with a peer took a more active role in the discussion, and when the children were given a test after the discussion, those who had been paired with a peer showed a higher level of moral reasoning. This suggests that moral development can be enhanced by interactions with peers and that social interaction is indeed important in moral development. The study by Peterson and Siegal (2002; see earlier) also supports Piaget's emphasis on the importance of peer interaction in the development of moral understanding.

As with his theory of cognitive development, Piaget has been criticised and his work has been developed by others. However, there does seem to be evidence for development of moral understanding and changes in the factors that influence moral decisions. So although there may be some disagreement with parts of his theory, Piaget made an important contribution to our comprehension of the development of children's understanding.

Kohlberg's stage theory of moral development

Kohlberg developed Piaget's ideas further. He produced an extended theory of moral development, going beyond childhood into adulthood.

His theory was much more complex and addressed some of the criticisms made of Piaget. However, there are some common characteristics of both theories.

- They are both stage models because they suggest that the development of moral understanding is a sequence of pre-determined innate stages.
- Each stage represents a development in thinking.
- The focus is not on *what* individuals are thinking but *how* they think and how this influences what judgements they make (i.e. moral behaviour) (Flanagan & Eysenck, 2000).

In this section of the chapter Kohlberg's stage model will be described and reviewed, and the empirical evidence for and against it will be discussed leading to an evaluation of the theory.

Kohlberg's theory consists of three levels of moral development and each level contains two stages, as illustrated in Figure 5.2. In Table 5.3 the major characteristics of each stage of Kohlberg's theory are described and the differences between the stages clearly identified.

If we return to the earlier example of the James Bulger case, we can apply Kohlberg's theory to this case, although it is more difficult to

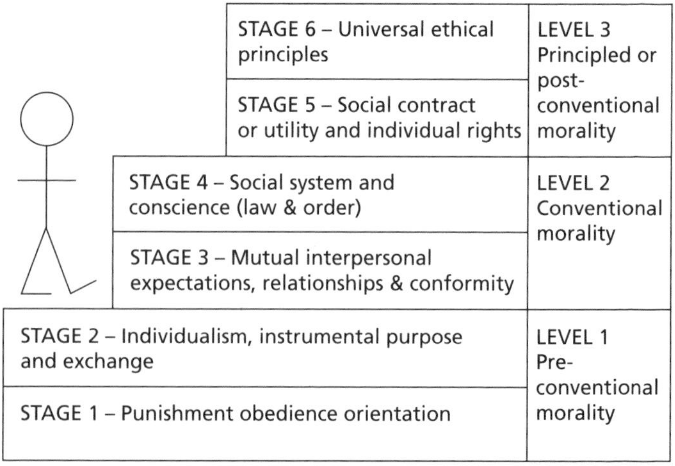

STAGE 6 – Universal ethical principles	LEVEL 3 Principled or post-conventional morality
STAGE 5 – Social contract or utility and individual rights	
STAGE 4 – Social system and conscience (law & order)	LEVEL 2 Conventional morality
STAGE 3 – Mutual interpersonal expectations, relationships & conformity	
STAGE 2 – Individualism, instrumental purpose and exchange	LEVEL 1 Pre-conventional morality
STAGE 1 – Punishment obedience orientation	

Figure 5.2 Kohlberg's stage theory of moral development

Table 5.3 Kohlberg's stage theory of moral development

Level 1 Pre-conventional morality	Level 2 Conventional morality	Level 3 Principled morality
This level is characterised by external authority – judgements of right and wrong are based on authority which is close and physically superior, e.g. parents. The standards by which actions are judged as right or wrong are external. The child uses the consequences of actions to decide what is right and what is wrong.	In this level there is a move away from external consequences to judgements based on the rules of the group to which the child belongs. The norms of the group are internalised.	At this level there is a move away from group rules to personal authority and personal choices based on individual principles and judgements.
Stage One In this stage children judge what is wrong by what gets punished, and what is right by what does not or is rewarded.	**Stage Three** In this stage good behaviour is what pleases others, trust is very valued as is loyalty. Maintaining relationships is seen as very important. Judgements about behaviour are made on the basis of intentions as well as actual behaviour.	**Stage Five** This stage sees the beginning of self-chosen principles. In this stage laws and rules are not relevant, what is right and fair is what is important.

continued . . .

Table 5.3 continued		
Level 1 **Pre-conventional** **morality**	**Level 2** **Conventional** **morality**	**Level 3** **Principled** **morality**
Stage Two In this stage the child behaves in a way that will be rewarded and avoids behaving in a way that will be punished. Right is seen to be what is fair, good is what brings pleasant results.	**Stage Four** Children focus upon larger social groups to provide them with moral norms. Moral reasoning focuses on duty and respect for authority, i.e. following laws and rules. Regulations are not questioned.	**Stage Six** In this final stage individuals assume responsibility for their own actions and decisions are based on principles of justice and respect for persons.

apply than Piaget's theory, as we cannot be sure at which stage the boys were, because Kohlberg did not attach ages to his stages. However, if we view the boys' behaviour it seems that they cannot have been operating at the pre-conventional stage of moral development. Children in this stage make moral judgements on the basis of what will be punished or rewarded, and their morals are externally determined – usually from their parents. Therefore if the boys were at this stage they would have been concerned about being punished and would have viewed the actions as wrong on the basis of their parents' moral judgements. It also seems that they cannot have been at the level of principled morality, as at this level individuals use principles of justice and fairness to make moral judgements and neither of these principles could apply to the killing of a small boy. Therefore it seems that the boys must have been at the conventional level of morality. Stage three appears to most accurately describe their level of moral development. In this stage maintaining relationships is viewed as important, as are trust and loyalty. These factors could explain why *two* boys could engage in such a crime. The fact that there were two may be significant, because their relationship to each other and their loyalty may have been important. Kohlberg suggests that these factors are influential in making moral judgements at this stage. Therefore an action may become morally acceptable if it helps to maintain a relationship, trust and loyalty.

Also at this stage intentions become influential in moral judgements. Kohlberg was interested in intentions not just the consequences of actions. Again Kohlberg's theory does not provide answers to the Jamie Bulger case, but the application of this theory may help to unravel the moral reasoning of the boys and suggest why they were able to act in a manner which most adults find inexplicable.

Empirical evidence

In support of Kohlberg

Kohlberg (1963) tested 10–16-year-old boys with a set of 10 moral dilemmas and then he asked them a series of questions to discover how they had arrived at their answers. An example of two of these dilemmas taken from Kohlberg's own work (1984, pp. 640–651) can be seen below.

Dilemma 1

Heinz and the druggist

In Europe, a woman was near death from a special kind of cancer. There was one drug that doctors thought might save her. It was a form of radium that a druggist in the same town had recently discovered. The drug was expensive to make, but the druggist was charging $2,000, or 10 times the cost of the drug, for a small (possibly life-saving) dose. Heinz, the sick woman's husband, borrowed all the money he could, about $1,000, or half of what he needed. He told the druggist that his wife was dying and asked him to sell the drug cheaper or let him pay later. The druggist replied, "No, I discovered the drug, and I'm going to make money from it." Heinz then became desperate and broke into the store to steal the drug for his wife.

Should Heinz have done that? Why or why not?

Dilemma 2

The tickets to the rock concert

Judy was a 12-year-old girl. Her mother promised her that she could go to a special rock concert coming to their town if she saved up from babysitting and lunch money to buy a ticket to the concert. She managed to save up the $15 the ticket cost plus another $5. But then her mother changed her mind and told Judy that she had to spend the money on new clothes for school. Judy was disappointed and decided to go to the concert anyway. She bought a ticket and told her mother that she had only been able to save $5. That Saturday she went to the performance and told her mother that she was spending the day with a friend. A week passed without her mother finding out. Judy then told her older sister, Louise, that she had gone to the performance and had lied to her mother about it. Louise wonders whether to tell their mother what Judy did.

Should Louise, the older sister, tell their mother that Judy lied about the money, or should she keep quiet? Why?

Kohlberg used the responses he obtained from the individuals that he interviewed to construct a classification scheme. Each individual was given a classification in terms of the stages outlined above for each of the 10 moral dilemmas they were given. For example, for dilemma 1 they were classified as IIa and for dilemma 2 they were classified as IIb. Kohlberg found that each individual emerged as predominantly belonging to one category. 10 year olds mainly showed stage 2 reasoning (some at stage 1 and 3); 16 year olds were mainly at stage 3.

The largest longitudinal study of moral reasoning was conducted by Colby et al. (1983). The researchers followed an original sample of 10-year-old boys until they were 36-year-old men. The research found that by age 22 stages 3 and 4 were dominant and stage 1 wasn't seen at all. This supported Kohlberg's theory of sequencing and development. In addition Colby et al. found that very few subjects missed a stage of development and that few regressed from higher to lower levels of reasoning during the course of the study.

Rest (1983b) conducted a review of 12 cross-sectional and longitudinal studies and his research found that participants generally developed moral reasoning as Kohlberg's theory suggested, thus providing support for Kohlberg's theory.

Kohlberg (1969) conducted a study of children in Britain, Taiwan, Turkey, USA and Yucatan (Mexico), and he found that the children showed similar sequences of development, suggesting that his theory was indeed a universal theory and applicable to different cultures (Edwards, 1980).

Thornton and Reid (1982) found adults who committed robberies were predominantly at stage 2 of reasoning – right is what brings reward.

In opposition to Kohlberg

Colby and Kohlberg (1987) surprisingly provide a critique of the model. They analysed their original data and found that less than 15% of the sample reached stage 5 and none reached stage 6. Siegal (1982) comments that 50% of Kohlberg's sample showed reasoning across two stages and thus the claims that they progressed and did not go back a stage seem questionable. Also it was clearly difficult to place individuals in just one stage of reasoning. Kohlberg argued that the problems were associated with the coding system used and not the theory.

Snarey (1985) reviewed 27 cross-cultural studies and found stages 1–4 at approximately the same ages in children from non-Western countries but minimal stage 5 reasoning and no stage 6. This suggests that this is a model which is culturally specific, and may not be able to applied to all cultures – see later section on culture.

Edwards (1980) comments that people in different cultures move through the stages that Kohlberg suggests at different rates and finish their moral development at different points. He states that in the USA most middle-class adults reach stage 4 and a small number stage 5. However, in some countries the individuals do not usually progress beyond stage 3. This again suggests that Kohlberg's notion of universality may be flawed and based on a Western model of morality (see later discussion of culture).

Gick (2003) argues against universal ethical norms and instead argues that morals actually develop and change because of individual perception and action. He states that moral behaviour becomes a moral rule when displayed by members of a society in a specific situation.

Thus he is arguing against the notion of universal morality and even suggesting that morals can be situationally specific.

It should also be noted that there is a noticeable absence of support for Kohlberg's original work. The assertions that Kohlberg made about the results of the Heinz interviews remain unsupported as the data remain unpublished. Also there are cultural biases in Kohlberg's findings – it appears that his designs and methods should be questioned, as his results seem to show that urban white Americans were the most morally developed group. He has been accused of creating a Western model of morality – see later discussion of culture.

Gilligan and Attanucci (1988) reviewed accounts of women's and men's own moral dilemmas and scored them. They found that men used a justice orientation predominantly and women used a care orientation, suggesting a gender difference that Kohlberg had overlooked. Kohlberg's major studies only used male participants.

Kohlberg and Krammer (1969) sought to address the issue of gender in a later study using both male and female participants. The results showed that women tended to have slightly lower levels of moral reasoning than men. This study shows two points, the first being that Kohlberg's claim for a universal theory is questionable if it is based solely on male participants and female participants score differently. Secondly the notion that women have lower levels of moral reasoning than men has been heavily criticised. The work of Gilligan will be discussed later – see section entitled Gender. Gilligan is an influential researcher who investigated the relationship between gender and morals.

Evaluation of Kohlberg's theory

Kohlberg developed a more detailed and complex theory than Piaget, which has generated research and sought to explain moral development from childhood through to adulthood. Piaget's model focused on children's moral development. Kohlberg used moral dilemmas recognising that people do not always behave consistently. Gibbs and Schnell (1985) criticised Kohlberg as testing moral reasoning, and they reiterated the problem that moral reasoning and moral behaviour don't always match.

However, Blasi (1980) reviewed 75 studies to investigate the relationship between moral behaviour and moral development, and found that there is a relationship between them. He noted that there are other factors which may be influential and these need to be recognised when trying to determine how an individual may behave in a moral situation. Richards et al. (1992) found that children at stage 1 or 3 of moral reasoning were less likely to be labelled as exhibiting conduct disorders than those at level 2. Kohlberg's theory would suggest that as children progress through the stages and their moral reasoning develops, so should their moral behaviour. This study disputes this, as children at stage 3 are more likely to exhibit problem behaviour than those at level 2. Birch (1998) suggests that the relationship between moral reasoning and moral behaviour is complex. Kohlberg's theory may have oversimplified the link. Therefore Kohlberg's theory may not be able to be used to predict behaviour – it is a theory of moral understanding but not of moral behaviour, which may limit its applications. However, Kohlberg did not ever claim to predict behaviour – he was interested in moral reasoning.

There is only a small amount of evidence for stages 5 and 6. Some individuals will never reach them. Later Kohlberg himself acknowledged that the sixth stage might not exist as a separate stage.

Kohlberg has been criticised for producing a male model of morality, which does not encompass female morality. Kohlberg has also been accused of creating a Western version of morality. He assumed that this morality is advanced, and ignored cultural variations. The issues of gender, culture and moral development will be discussed in detail later in this chapter. Kohlberg, like Piaget, did not take account of the influence of emotion on moral reasoning and behaviour.

In Table 5.4 a comparison of the theories of Piaget and Kohlberg can be seen. An alternative explanation for the development of moral understanding is Eisenberg's theory of pro-social reasoning, which is described next.

Progress exercise

1. What methods did Piaget use to investigate moral development in children?

2. Detail one study which has been used to dispute Kohlberg's theory of moral development.

Table 5.4 A comparison of Kohlberg's and Piaget's theories of moral development

Piaget	Kohlberg
Both thought that the developmental of moral understanding occurred in recognisable stages and developed stage models to describe this development. The models have close similarities, for example the importance of authority in early moral development and judgements based on intention in later moral development.	
Theory included three stages of moral development.	Theory included three stages but six sub-stages.
Both saw moral development as linked to cognitive development.	
Used moral stories in pairs and asked children to judge behaviour of children in story.	Used moral dilemmas, rather than pairs of stories.
Peer interaction seen as important for development of moral understanding.	Development of moral understanding not based on interaction.
Theory focused on children's moral development.	Theory described moral development through childhood to adulthood.
Both assumed link between moral judgements and behaviour.	
Both criticised for failing to see gender and culture as important influential factors in moral development.	

Eisenberg's model of pro-social reasoning

One of the criticisms of both Piaget's and Kohlberg's work is that it is based around rule breaking or morally wrong behaviour. For example, in both moral stories and moral dilemmas children behave wrongly or break rules. However moral development is also about making appropriate or correct moral decisions and behaving in a morally appropriate way. Eisenberg was particularly interested in this aspect of moral development and she used the term **pro-social behaviour** – this is behaviour which is intended to help another individual. Sharing and co-operative behaviours have often been studied as part of pro-social behaviour.

Eisenberg used the idea of moral stories or dilemmas but in her particular type of stories children were asked to choose between behaviour which is self-centred, and behaviour which helps another person.

An example of Eisenberg's moral dilemmas
A child is on the way to a party when he finds another child who has fallen over and hurt himself. If the child who is going to the party stops to help the injured child he will miss the party. What should he do?

In this story the child is not asked to make a judgement about another child's behaviour but to think about how another child should behave. The child can choose to stop and help the injured child at a personal cost – missing the party – or they can take the self-interest approach and choose to go to the party. This kind of dilemma allows the child to take either a pro-social approach to the problem or a more self-centred approach. Eisenberg's dilemmas allowed children to choose to behave pro-socially, unlike those presented by Kohlberg and Piaget where the focus was on morally wrong behaviour. Eisenberg, like Piaget and Kohlberg, found a developmental sequence and developed a model of pro-social reasoning with six stages (a stage theory). This model is shown in Figure 5.3. Table 5.5 describes the main characteristics of the stages of Eisenberg's model and clearly differentiates between the stages.

Like Piaget and Kohlberg, Eisenberg saw a clear link between the development of moral reasoning and the maturation of cognitive

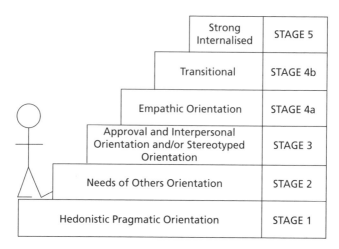

Figure 5.3 **Eisenberg's stage model of pro-social reasoning**

Table 5.5 *Eisenberg's stage model of pro-social reasoning*

Stage 1

Children make moral judgements on the basis of their own selfish goals. 'Good behaviour' is what meets their needs. We can see that in the story described in the text a child could answer 'I would go to the party' as this meets their own needs. Equally they could say 'I would stop' but the reason is 'because I might need them to help me at

Stage 2

Concern for needs of other even though in conflict with own needs.

Stage 3

Moral thinking is based on stereotypical views of how 'good' and 'bad' people usually behave. Again if we return to the earlier example a child might answer 'I would stop and help because it's the right thing to do. Because I am a good person.'

continued . . .

Table 5.5 continued

some point'. So they
do not stop out of a
sense of helping the
child but because they
might need help.
This typifies this stage
of pro-social
reasoning.

Stage 4a	Stage 4b	Stage 5
Signs of concern for other people. Feeling of guilt or positive feelings in relation to own behaviour.	Evidence of internalised values.	Strong evidence of internalised values. Concern to meet responsibilities in relation to society and individuals. Here the answer to the party dilemma might be 'I would stop, it's our duty to treat others as we want to be treated. Everyone has the right to help.' Strong conviction about individual rights and equality of all people.

abilities in general. Eisenberg also emphasised the development of role-taking skills. That is, as children develop, their ability to see things from the perspective of others increases and this is an important part of moral development. As children develop these skills, their sense of empathy and understanding for others increases and therefore there is an increase in their pro-social behaviour. As they understand the needs of others they can make decisions which do not always benefit themselves.

Empirical evidence

In support of Eisenberg

Eisenberg found evidence for her stages across West Germany, Italy and Poland. Eisenberg-Berg and Hand (1979) found that when pre-school children were presented with Eisenberg's dilemmas they tended to be quite self-centred in their responses. In the party example provided, they might say that the child should go to the party because otherwise he will miss out on the fun. Older children were able to take account of the feelings of the other child. These findings supported Eisenberg's theory.

The same children used in the above study were tested on a variety of different moral dilemmas and the researchers found that children's moral understanding was inconsistent. Pre-school children discussed the dilemmas and mentioned how they would feel in the situation but also how the other child would feel, showing signs of two stages of pro-social reasoning. When the children were tested a year later they showed signs of development in their moral reasoning and gave less self-centred responses and more pro-social ones, indicating a development consistent with Eisenberg's theory. In a further longitudinal study Eisenberg et al. (1987; Eisenberg & Fabes, 1991) has followed a group of children beginning at the age of 4 and finishing when they reached adolescence. The results reflected and provided further support for Eisenberg's stage model.

Support for Eisenberg's focus on the importance of role-taking comes from research conducted by Caplan and Hay (1989). Their research observed children between the ages of 3 and 5. These children were seen to be upset when another child was upset, but the watching children did not often offer support or help. This supports Eisenberg's theory that initially young children find it difficult to role-take and so although they recognise the emotion they are unable to imagine what the person needs and therefore to help. Young children assume an adult will provide support – older children realise that they can help; an adult is not always required.

Midlarsky and Hannah (1985) found that older children were more likely to share than younger children.

Peterson (1983) found that younger children were just as capable as older children of being helpful if it was made clear to them that they were capable and able to help. This contradicts Eisenberg's model, which shows age differences in pro-social behaviour and suggests that younger children tend to be less altruistic.

Fraver and Bransletter (1994) stated that age differences in sharing and helping were not supported when the research was conducted in a natural setting and not a laboratory setting, suggesting that age differences may be a result of the method used to investigate pro-social behaviour and not a result of real differences.

Radke-Yarrow and Zahn Waxler (1984) conducted a study of pro-social behaviour. They asked mothers to record their infant's behaviour every day over a period of several months. The researchers wanted to investigate the infants' reactions to another person in distress, therefore some events were staged, for example someone pretended to be injured and someone pretended to be angry on the phone. They found that a large percentage of children behaved in a pro-social manner. Young children only showed empathetic distress and cried when the incidents occurred. However, many older toddlers tried to help. Their help was not always appropriate, such as trying to feed someone who was hurt! But it was well intentioned all the same.

Eisenberg might disagree with the interpretation of this study; she would suggest that the crying in younger children supports her idea that they are unable to understand how to help. However, the study did illustrate that older toddlers can show altruistic behaviour. In Peterson's (1983) research, children required adult intervention to recognise their helping abilities.

It can be seen that Eisenberg approached moral development from a different viewpoint than Kohlberg and Piaget. She saw moral development as being about making pro-social choices as much as moral judgements and about including pro-social behaviour. Her model suggested that differences in this kind of behaviour are related to cognitive development. Some research questions her assumptions about young children's altruistic tendencies, but she has provided an alternative account of moral development and raised the important issue of pro-social behaviour as part of moral development. Eisenberg's theory therefore progressed the study of moral development, but two key issues still remain. These are the influence of gender and culture.

Gender and moral development

The issue of gender and moral development has created much debate. Are there differences in moral development, moral behaviour and moral judgements which are determined by or related to gender? Are males and females different as regards their morals?

Holstein (1976) found that adolescent boys were mostly at stage 4 and adolescent girls at stage 3. Does this mean girls are morally inferior to boys? Understandably many have argued against this. One of the main researchers in this area is Gilligan.

Gilligan

Carol Gilligan suggested that Kohlberg's model was a 'male' model of morality (not surprising since the research involved interviews with boys only) and that it was biased against females. She suggested that there were two main and distinct **moral orientations** – the basis on which you make moral decisions. These are justice and care. Justice involves not being unfair; care involves responsibility to those in need. Gilligan (1982) found differences in moral understanding between boys and girls. Boys tended to make moral judgements based on what was right or just. Girls, however, were not as concerned with justice but their judgements were more concerned with moral 'care' and responsibility. Therefore their concern was with the effect on people and not what was just. In a study in 1982 Gilligan interviewed 29 American women who were pregnant as they were involved in a 'real-life' dilemma, whether to continue with their pregnancies or to have an abortion. From her study she identified three stages of moral reasoning, which shared some similarities with Kohlberg's model. Gilligan created a stage model of moral development.

- Stage 1: Reasoning in terms of self-interest. What was best for the individual and their needs were put above the needs of others.
- Stage 2: Self-sacrifice – sacrifice own concerns for welfare of others.
- Stage 3: Non-violence – avoid hurting others.

In a later study (Gilligan & Attanucci, 1988) Gilligan again found that generally men favoured a justice orientation and women a care orientation. But both genders had elements of both orientations.

Evidence for gender differences in moral situations has been supported by Tibbetts (1999) who found clear gender differences in a study investigating test cheating. Gilligan suggested that society expects females to be caring and therefore this is their moral orientation. She claimed that women are socialised into being caring and nurturing and men are socialised into being more detached and independent. She suggested that this had led to a male model of morality based upon justice and abstract moral principles and a female model based on care-orientation and welfare. Recent theories about gender and genetics suggest there may have been evolutionary pressures that led females to be caring and sharing whereas men are not; women 'tend and befriend' (and thus cope better with stress) but this would lead them to only achieve level 3 of Kohlberg's stages, and men appear morally superior.

Gilligan characterised this model as a model of care not justice. If her model is used, men can appear morally inferior. However, there is evidence against these gender differences. Humphries, Parker and Jagers (2000) also found gender differences in moral reasoning but interestingly found that boys used empathy as part of their moral reasoning. This suggests that although differences may exist, Gilligan may not be correct in her statements about what is male or female moral understanding. Gilligan argued that females and not males used empathy in their moral reasoning.

Luedecke, Zirkel and Beck (1998) suggest that Gilligan's assumption that men and women follow different moral principles cannot be supported and that moral principles are also affected by the social situation, the individual's self and their moral competence. This article questions Gilligan's notion of different moral principles for males and females.

Rest (1983b) suggests that Gilligan has exaggerated the effect of gender on Kohlberg's stage model. Walker (1984) found no consistent differences between genders on Kolhberg's moral dilemmas, suggesting that the differences between the morality of the genders that Gilligan claims, may not exist.

Eisenberg et al. (1987) found that girls between the ages of 10 and 12 were more caring and empathic than boys. Lyons (1983) found that males were more likely to use a justice orientation and females a care orientation.

Gilligan's model is based on a social constructionist model. That is, that gender roles are socially constructed. As these roles change, the model could and is likely to become outdated. Also as the roles and socialisation of males and females are different in different cultures, Gilligan's model may only be appropriate for this culture, now, and may not endure or be universally appropriate. The controversy over gender differences and moral development seems certain to continue, but Gilligan's work was extremely important in raising the issue of gender. Culture is another issue which must be discussed in relation to moral development.

Culture

Earlier in this chapter, a critique of Kohlberg was provided. This included the point that Kohlberg's theory has been criticised for being based on Western culture. There are two common cultural distinctions. These are collectivist and individualistic cultures. Collectivist cultures value family, interdependence, sharing and responsibility. Individualistic cultures value independence and individuality. Children growing up in these different cultures encounter very different values and therefore we might expect that their moral development would also be different. One child may place value on helping others (a collectivist approach) more than doing what is best in a situation (an individualist approach). Kohlberg failed to address such cultural differences.

Simpson (1974) felt that Kohlberg's model is based on a Western model of morality and then applied to non-Western cultures without consideration of any differences. Whiting and Whiting (1975) compared Kenyan and American children on altruistic behaviour. They found only 8% of American children showed such selfless helping behaviour as opposed to 100% of Kenyan children. Miller and Bersoff (1992) conducted a cross-cultural study. They used a sample of Americans and a sample of Indians to investigate if cultural differences in morality existed, by presenting the subjects with moral situations, which dealt with breaking laws or breaking rules of relationships. They found that Indians tended to resolve problems by concentrating on the relationships between people, and Americans tended to use justice as a solution rather than interpersonal choices. The research suggests that this reflects cultural differences in assessing moral behaviour and therefore moral reasoning is connected to culture.

Mones and Haswell (1998) furthered this discussion by suggesting that a child's family teaches the child cultural moral values and thus acts as a 'family culture'. Again this study emphasises the importance of culture in the development of moral reasoning and suggests a reason why different children develop different moral values. The argument could be developed to state that not only do different cultures develop different moral reasoning, but also different families create different moral values. For example, some families think smoking is right – others that it is wrong. This kind of research argues against Kohlberg's ideas that the development of moral reasoning is universal.

Hedge and Yousif (1992) did not find cultural differences when comparing British and Sudanese people on the issue of helpfulness. However, Snarey (1985) conducted a review of 44 studies in 26 cultures and found support across these cultures for Kohlberg's theory.

Schewdar (1990) suggests that different cultures might have different moral rules and realities that are a result of different histories, traditions and cultural rules. He suggests that Kohlberg failed to take the importance of culture into account.

Miller and Bersoff (1992) suggest that motivations for adhering to different rules might differ across cultures in important ways. In their study they used a sample of 120 subjects from the USA and from a city in southern India. The US group held mainly Christian and Jewish views, and the Indian group mainly Hindu views. The participants were presented with situations where there were breaches of justice or interpersonal relations. There were clear differences between the two groups. The Indian more frequently resolved problems in terms of dealing with relations between people, whereas the Americans used justice as a way to solve problems. The researchers suggested that part of the Indian culture is based around obligations to others and there is much more emphasis on this than in the American culture. The research led them to argue that culture has real influence on the development of moral understanding. In addition they argued that it is incorrect for Kohlberg to assume that the kind of reasoning used by the Indians is inferior to that used by the Americans.

Other research conducted by Miller, Bersoff and Harwood (1990) also used a sample of Indian and American subjects and showed that there were other differences in their moral reasoning based on culture. In one study participants were given a number of scenarios ranging from life-threatening events to minor events in which a person dependent on them was involved. The participants had to state whether they would feel an obligation to help. All participants felt an obligation to help in life-threatening situations but the Indians kept a consistent view of moral obligation whatever the situation, whereas the Americans did not – their obligation levels reduced as the severity of the situation reduced. The researchers again claimed that this difference in moral obligation was due to cultural differences – caring for the needs of others is an important part of the Indian culture and this affects the morals of people reared in that culture.

A further study by Bersoff and Miller (1993) asked participants to make a moral judgement regarding the question of justice. Again a series of scenarios were presented, of acts performed under anger or fear, in accidents and poor behaviour of a 10 year old. Indian culture places emphasis on situational influences, so it was expected that Indians would be less harsh in their judgements of acts committed under fear or anger, or in an accident. However, the results showed little difference between the two cultures. All participants judged the poor behaviour of the 10 year old as wrong and absolved individuals of guilt if they acted because of fear or anger, or in an accident. This suggests that some overlap between moral values of different cultures exists and that not all morals are culturally determined.

It may indeed not be the case that all moral judgement and reasoning is culturally determined. Helwig, Tisak, and Turiel 1990 suggest that individuals across many cultures find the idea of torture or child abuse abhorrent. Thus, as with Miller and Bersoff, it cannot be argued that all moral rules are culturally determined.

Emler (1987) suggests that Kohlberg's theory is **ethnocentric**, reflecting male Western values, and that it fails to take account of any conceptions of reality that do not fit into the theory. Again this is an area of controversy and subject to continuing research, but the influence of a collectivist or individualist society is likely to impact the development of moral understanding.

Summary

Piaget's stage theory of moral development was built upon research into game playing and moral stories. The stages were pre-moral judgement, moral realism and moral subjectivism. There is a degree of empirical support for Piaget, in particular for the notion of a sequence of moral development but criticisms of his theory include underestimating children's ability, and unrealistic and confusing dilemmas and memory problems.

Kohlberg developed Piaget's work and constructed a stage model made up of six stages. Again there is empirical evidence in support of Kohlberg's model. Kohlberg sought to develop a model which was universal and described cognitive development from childhood to adulthood. He based his work around the use of moral dilemmas. Kohlberg and Piaget thought that moral development was linked to general cognitive development. However, Kohlberg has been criticised for creating a model based on a male Western version of moral development, which ignores gender and culture differences.

Eisenberg developed a model of pro-social reasoning. There were six stages to her model and there are some similarities between her model and Kohlberg's. However, Eisenberg thought that Piaget and Kohlberg had wrongly concentrated on rule breaking to learn about moral development, and she felt that moral development was as much about making positive or pro-social choices as it was about rule breaking.

Gilligan investigated the influence of gender and created her own stage model based on research. She suggested a distinction between a justice orientation (predominantly male) and a care orientation (predominantly female). This area is still controversial.

Finally it is likely that culture may affect moral development and there is some empirical support for differences between collectivist and individualistic societies.

1. Describe Kohlberg's theory of the development of moral understanding.

2. Evaluate Piaget's theory with reference to empirical studies.

Further reading

Carpendale, J.I.M. (2000). Kohlberg and Piaget on stages and moral reasoning. *Developmental Review*, *20*, 181–205. This is a detailed article really analysing and evaluating Piaget's and Kohlberg's theories in depth. It will help readers who wish to fully develop their critical understanding.

6

Study aids

IMPROVING YOUR ESSAY-WRITING SKILLS

At this point in the book you have acquired the knowledge necessary to tackle the exam itself. Answering exam questions is a skill that this chapter shows you how to improve. Examiners obviously have first-hand knowledge about what goes wrong in exams. For example, candidates frequently do not answer the question which has been set, rather they answer the one they hoped would come up. Or they do not make effective use of the knowledge they have but just 'dump their psychology' on the page and hope the examiner will sort it out for them. A grade 'C' answer usually contains appropriate material but tends to be limited in detail and commentary. To lift such an answer to a grade 'A' or 'B' may require no more than a little more detail, better use of material and coherent organisation. It is important to appreciate it may not involve writing at any greater length, but rather necessitate the elimination of passages which do not add to the quality of the answer and some elaboration of those which do.

The essays given here are notionally written by an 18-year-old in 30 minutes and marked bearing that in mind. It is important when writing to such a tight limit that you make every sentence count. Each essay in this chapter is followed by detailed comments about its strengths and weaknesses. The most common problems to watch out for are:

- Failure to answer the question set and instead reproducing a model answer to a similar question which you have pre-learned.
- Not delivering the right balance between description and evaluation analysis.
- Writing 'everything you know' about a topic in the hope that something will get credit and the examiner will sort your work out for you. Remember that excellence demands selectivity, so improvements can often be made by removing material that is irrelevant to the question set and elaborating material which is relevant.
- Failing to use your material effectively. It is not enough to place the information on the page, you must also show the examiner that you are using it to make a particular point.

Practice essay 1

Outline Piaget's theory of cognitive development. (12 marks)

Candidate's answer

Cognitive development can be referred to as the development of thinking. Piaget researched a lot into cognitive development, especially on young children and babies. He believed that everyone is born with a set of schema, which are simple building blocks of knowledge. In his theory, as babies grow so do their schema. As the child develops, it progresses through a number of stages of cognitive development. He developed a stage model where each stage followed from the previous one and showed a development in thinking and understanding. The stages were sensorimotor, pre-operational, concrete and formal operational. Each stage was related to specific ages. As well as these four stages, Piaget included egocentrism in his theory. This is to view things from other people's perspectives. Piaget carried out an experiment into this called 'The Swiss Mountain Experiment', which tested young children's abilities of egocentrism. He set up a scene of three mountains with one mountain holding a house, one a cross and the other had snow on it. He then placed a doll on the scene and asked the children what the doll would be able to see when it was put in specific places.

The results showed that young children were unable to see the experiment from any perspective than their own and they answered what they could see. Older children were able to answer what the doll could see showing that they were not egocentric and had progressed in their thinking.

Conservation was another part of his theory into cognitive development. This is the understanding of a quantity of something even if it has had a physical change, for example, liquid. Piaget stated that young children were unable to understand the concepts of reversibility and compensation. This meant that they were unable to conserve. He tested children's ability to conserve volume, mass, liquid and number. Piaget believed that at a certain age, children would be able to conserve. He tested this using young children and amounts of liquid in different shaped beakers. He would then ask them which had the most/least amount in it. Young children in the pre-operational stage were unable to answer correctly but older children in the concrete operational stage were able to conserve. Again showing a development in thinking. Piaget thought that children's cognitive development was linked to the natural maturation of the brain and therefore children had to be developmentally ready to learn things. Piaget's theory had a lot of educational implications.

These are all parts of Piaget's theory into cognitive development.

Examiner's comments

This essay would receive a mark of 7 out of 12. It does discuss the stage model of cognitive development and list the stages, although there is no description of what each stage includes. There needs to be more detail of the characteristics and contents of each stage. The candidate mentions the fact that the stages are associated with ages but does not state the age range associated with each stage. Also the concepts of conservation and egocentrism are described and explained. However there is no mention of accommodation, assimilation or equilibration. There is mention of educational implications but no specific details of what they are. The essay addresses some of the main issues of Piaget's theory but does not describe Piaget's ideas about children as active thinkers and different from adult thinkers. It needed to be more detailed and present a clearer description of the theory.

Practice essay 2

To what extent can this theory explain the development of thinking? (12 marks)

Candidate's answer

Piaget was criticised by other psychologists for the methods he used in his experiments and the theory behind it. Piaget had no real scientific evidence that proved that schemas actually existed, so this idea was purely based on his thoughts rather than facts. Piaget did many experiments to back his theory up about the four stages of cognitive development, however he has been criticised for underestimating children's abilities at the ages he included in his theory. Yet, a lot of his work has proved to be useful for other psychologists to look into.

Piaget's 'Swiss Mountain Experiment', into egocentrism found that a large percentage of the children who were tested could not give an answer as to what the doll could see from certain points in the scene. This immediately made Piaget think that the children at the age he tested mustn't have an egocentric ability. However, this may have purely been because the method used was far too advanced and complicated for the children to understand. Other researchers have modified his experiment and found different results. Again, with his conservation idea, Piaget has been criticised for underestimating a child's ability at doing the task because he didn't make the tests easy enough for them to understand.

Despite all this, psychologists have furthered a lot of Piaget's work in cognitive development and still quite a few of his concepts are used today in society and seen as right.

Examiner's comments

This essay would receive a mark of 6/12. The student addresses some of the problems with Piaget's theory and some of the weaknesses with his methods and experiments. However, to fully answer the question the student would need to think about the limitations of Piaget's theory; some of these are undoubtedly the weaknesses in design and his conclusions. The work of Vygotsky could be used to provide a discussion of the limitations of Piaget's theory. A discussion of the importance of language and culture in cognitive development could have been provided. Also it is important that the positive aspects of Piaget's theory are discussed. There is some recognition of this. Piaget did make a contribution to our understanding of children's cognitive development. He introduced the idea that children thought differently from adults, that they were active learners, that their thinking was developed in stages and that children's cognitive development was dependent on maturation. These factors could have been included to make a more detailed answer to the question.

Practice essay 3

How does Piaget's theory describe the development of moral understanding? (12 marks)

Candidate's answer

Piaget believed that moral development was linked with his studies into cognitive development as he thought that it was to do with the children's cognitive abilities in the first place. He believed that children could be put into different stages depending on how old they were. He also believes that once a child starts socialising with friends without parents there, they begin to think and develop on their own. Piaget saw peers as important in the development of morals. He carried out studies in 1932, which explained and gave evidence for his theory in more detail. This involved three groups of children at different ages playing a game of marbles. He observed how they played and found that at different ages they changed the rules of the game depending on how far developed they were in moral understanding. At the youngest age he observed, the children played using no rules. At the age of 5, those children played the game using rules, which they didn't change in any way at all. At age 10, the children didn't stick to the rules and altered them to suit themselves. He also used moral stories where children were given pairs of stories and asked which child had been the naughtiest. Piaget was interested in their reasoning. He found that younger children judged on consequences and older children on intention. He developed a stage theory of moral development like his stage theory of cognitive development where every stage built

117

upon the one before. Piaget though that children's moral development occurred in stages and that each stage represented a development in moral reasoning and thinking. These stages were pre-moral judgement, moral realism and moral relativity.

Examiner's comment

This essay would get a mark of 7/12 as the candidate has stated that Piaget developed a stage model and that each stage represented a development in moral understanding. The stages are named but not described – there needed to be a much more detailed description of each stage and the kind of reasoning associated with the stages. Also the methods Piaget used to develop his theory are described but the essay question does not ask about methods. These are important but the main focus of the essay needed to be on the question about how Piaget's theory describes moral development. Again the essential elements are here but the essay requires development.

Practice essay 4

Evaluate Piaget's theory with reference to relevant studies. (12 marks)

Candidate's answer

Piaget (1932) used a game of marbles to test children's moral development and to see how they kept to rules and if they changed them. He found that younger children were not able to understand rules, older children stuck to the rules and said they couldn't be broken and older children still recognised the rules but thought they could be changed if everyone agreed. This supported Piaget's theory of development and his three stages. Piaget also used moral stories to investigate children's moral development. He presented them with pairs of stories. In one a child called John knocked over 25 cups unintentionally and a child called Henry broke one while being naughty. Piaget asked the children who was naughtier. Young children answered the one who broke 25 cups as they judged by consequence, older children answered the child who intended to be naughty – they judged by intention, again supporting Piaget's theory. However, Ferguson & Rule conducted a study where they asked children who was naughtier, a child who pushed another off the wall bars wanted to do a lot of harm and one who only wanted to do a little harm. In opposition to Piaget they found young children did judge by intention. Laupa (1991) carried out a study that asked children whether they would do something wrong if an adult said it was OK, even young children stated that they wouldn't, that it would still be wrong. Again this contradicted Piaget's view that young children see adults as moral authorities and that adults moral decisions can't be questioned. Therefore there is a lot of research in support of Piaget but also a lot of research that questions Piaget's theory and his original findings.

Examiner's comments

This essay would receive a mark of 7/12 as there is support for Piaget and opposition to his theory. The studies used either support or question key aspects of his theory. There are many more studies that could and should have been discussed. The only support for Piaget comes from his own work and there are other studies that support his original findings and these needed to be discussed. It is important to include dates with studies. Also it may be useful to state what aspects have been supported and which aspects have been questioned. The essay provides arguments in support of and in opposition to Piaget and this is how it needed to be written. However it needed to be more detailed and developed.

KEY RESEARCH SUMMARIES

Study 1

Piaget, J. & Inhelder, B. (1969) The pendulum experiment. In *The Psychology of the child* (pp. 147–148) London: Routledge.

Aim

The aim of this study was to investigate how children solved logic problems and to identify the strategies they used to reach a solution. Piaget and Inhelder were interested to see whether children of different ages approached the problem differently, as Piaget's model of cognitive development would suggest, and thus provide evidence for this model.

Method

Piaget and Inhelder presented children with a problem to solve. The children were presented with a pendulum – a piece of string and a weight on the end. They had to work out what factor affected the speed of the swing of the pendulum. They were able to change the length of the string and the size of the weight. Children were observed while trying to solve the problem, and records of the strategies and approaches that they used were taken. Also a record was taken of their explanations for strategies and their explanations of what factor was influential in the speed of the swing. Samples of children aged between 5 and adolescence were used, and all were given the same problem and the same materials. This method allowed Piaget and Inhelder to study the different strategies employed by the different age groups.

Results

Piaget and Inhelder found that children in the concrete operational stage of development were convinced that varying the weight was the influential factor in the speed of the swing. Children in this stage did not use a systematic approach but varied the length of string and the weight at the same time, making it difficult to identify the key factor. They used a random approach to solving the problem. These children found it difficult to exclude the weight factor. When they varied the length of the string and the weight at the same time they provided reasons for the weight being the important factor each time. The children found it difficult to move from their original theory on the importance of the weight, which Piaget stated is also the first theory adults use, to an investigation of the importance of the length of the string.

Children in the formal operational period – pre-adolescents – were able to separate the two factors and to review the influence of each factor separately. They were able to solve the problem by a series of logical tests, which first changed the weight on the end while maintaining the length, and then maintained the weight and changed the length of string, or vice versa. They demonstrated a systematic approach to problem solving and were able to solve the problem.

This study provided evidence for Piaget's model of cognitive development. The results illustrated that children in the concrete operational period were unable to use a logical and systematic approach to problem solving but adopted a random approach, which would not lead them to a solution. Children in the formal operational period were using a systematic approach to solve the problem, which again supports Piaget's stage model.

The description of the research does not provide a clear indication of the number of children used or the method of observation and recording of results. This makes it difficult to judge the validity of the claims made.

Also other researchers have questioned the experimental design. Bryant and Trabasso (1971) stated that children's inability to solve the problem was not due to their lack of problem-solving skills or strategies but to the limitations of memory in young children. Children may have tried to use a systematic approach but they were unable to remember the solutions they had tried before. This might make it look as if they were using a random approach. However, Piaget and Inhelder found that young children consistently concentrated on the weight, suggesting that they were not able to use strategies that tested all factors.

Danner and Day (1977) suggested that children could be trained to solve such puzzles. If children were taught the strategies to use and how to approach problems in a logical manner, they could solve such problems. This idea contradicts Piaget's claim that children in the concrete operational stage are unable to use such reasoning. However, the fact that children need to be taught such approaches suggests that it is not a natural ability during this stage of development, supporting Piaget's original ideas. This study has therefore provided evidence for differences in problem-solving strategies in children in the pre-operational and concrete operational stages of development, lending support to Piaget's theory. As with much of Piaget's research, questions about experimental design have been raised.

Study 2

Blaye, A., Light, P., Joiner, R. & Sheldon, S. (1991) Collaboration as a facilitator of planning and problem solving on a computer based task. *British Journal of Educational Psychology, 61,* 471–483.

Aim

The researchers wanted to investigate whether peer tutoring could increase individual ability at computer tasks, and therefore to investigate the effect of peer tutoring.

Method

The researchers used a sample of 11-year-old children. Some of the children worked on the computers alone, others worked in pairs. They were trying to solve problems which were presented in a computer game. The problems were very difficult. The researchers recorded which children solved the problems, and were especially interested to see whether pairs of children shared knowledge and therefore helped each other to solve problems. The children took part in three different tests and the results of each were recorded.

Results

The results showed that on the first test no child was able to complete the problems when working alone. Some of the pairs completed the problems, but not all. On the second test approximately 50% of the pairs completed the problems and 20% of those working alone. In the third test all children worked alone. The results of this test indicated that over 70% of children who had previously worked in pairs were able to complete the test, but only 30% of children who had worked as individuals throughout.

Discussion

The study supports the idea of peer tutoring, which was seen as important by Vygotsky. Those children who worked together seemed to learn from each other and indeed to develop their thinking while discussing the problem. Children working alone did not have the benefit of the knowledge of the other child or of new knowledge that might be constructed through discussion. Therefore peer tutoring can be seen to encourage children to move from their current level of problem-solving ability to a more advanced level, to move through their ZPD as suggested by Vygotsky. However, some of the children who worked together were not successful in the final test, suggesting that peer tutoring did not have a universal positive effect. Also some children working alone without the benefit of peer tutoring were successful, suggesting that it is possible to move through the ZPD without peer tutoring. The task must also be taken into account – some of these children would have been used to computers and computer programs, and these children may have been at an advantage at the beginning of the study, which may account for the individual success rate. Also the intellectual ability of the children is not accounted for. More studies need to be conducted involving a range of problems of different types to fully investigate the role of peer tutoring. However, this study does lend support to Vygotsky's theory and in particular to the idea of peer tutoring.

Study 3

Horn, J.M. (1983). Texas Adoption Project: Adopted children and their intellectual resemblance to biological and adoptive parents. *Child Development, 54*, 266–275.

Aim

The aim of this large-scale project was to investigate the nature–nurture debate about the development of measured intelligence. The researchers wanted to identify whether genetic influences or environmental influences were more influential in the development of intelligence.

Method

The data for the study were derived from an adoption agency in Texas. The IQ scores of 469 children were taken; all of these children had been adopted soon after birth into a total of 300 families, as some siblings were adopted together. The IQ scores of the biological mothers for each child were available; all of these mothers were unmarried when the children were adopted. The IQ scores of the adoptive mothers were also made available. The researchers compared the IQ scores of the children with those of both their adoptive mothers and their biological mothers. Correlations of the scores were produced.

Results

A correlation of 0.28 was found between biological mothers' IQ scores and those of their children. A correlation of 0.15 was found between those of adoptive mothers and their children. These results suggested some genetic influence in the development of intelligence, as the correlation was higher between biological mothers and children than between adoptive mothers and children.

Discussion

There are several weaknesses with this study. It was a large-scale study but the sample only used unmarried mothers, which may have produced biased results. Also the study took place in Texas and it would be useful to conduct a similar study in another country to investigate the influence of culture. Stoolmiller (1998) questioned elements of the design of this study and suggested that there was a large underestimation of the effect of the shared family environment. However, this criticism was later disputed by Loehlin and Horn (2000). It is necessary to revisit the issues with IQ tests because, as stated in Chapter 4, they have been heavily criticised for being culturally biased, for only measuring certain aspects of intelligence and for only pro-viding a snapshot measure of intelligence. (For a more detailed discussion of this point see Chapter 4, Intelligence tests and bias.) If the tests are flawed then any conclusions drawn on the basis of these test results are open to question.

This study provided some evidence for the influence of genetics in determining IQ, as the children's scores were more closely related to their biological parents than their adoptive parents. These results suggested that genetics had a stronger influence on the development of intelligence. However, the difference between the correlations is quite small and neither correlation is high, suggesting that other factors are more influential than those measured. A correlation of 1 is a perfect correlation, so these results indicate that 80% of the variability in intelligence scores is unaccounted for, suggesting that environmental factors are important.

Study 4

Damon, W. & Killen, M. (1992). The influence of peer interaction and the process of change in children's moral reasoning. *Merrill-Palmer Quarterly*, *28*, 347–367. In P.K. Smith, H. Cowie & M. Blades. *Understanding Children's Development*, 3rd Edition. Oxford: Blackwell, 1998.

Aim

The aim of this study was first to investigate whether peer interaction would result in an increase in levels of moral reasoning. (This was part of Piaget's theory of moral development – he emphasised the importance of peers in the development of moral reasoning.) The second aim was to identify whether certain kinds of interaction could be connected to such changes in moral reasoning.

Method

A total of 147 children aged between 5 and 8 years were used as the sample. They all attended public school in the USA. The interview used was Damon's positive justice interview; this was used as a measure of moral reasoning. The interview was given before the test and about three and a half months after the test. Children were placed into three groups – the experimental group, who engaged in peer debates, and two control groups, one in which children individually discussed a moral problem with the experimenter and the other group who did not.

About two months after the initial interview children in the experimental group were placed into groups of three and a fourth, younger, child was placed with them. They were asked to make bracelets from beads and string. The youngest child always made the fewest bracelets. This child was called away, and after a few more comments by the experimenter the children were given ten sweet bars and asked to decide how to share them out between the four children who had taken part. The discussion that then took place between the peers was recorded onto video and it was scored for the content of the discussion of each child. The children in the control group came on their own and discussed a similar problem about justice.

Results

The results indicated that the experimental group showed more change in their moral reasoning than the control group. Children who had been using lower levels of moral reasoning were more likely to show improvements in their level, especially if they were active in the discussion both in terms of input of ideas and response from other group members. Children who began the test with high levels of moral reasoning did not show advances in their moral reasoning even if they were active participants.

Discussion

The results of this experiment do lend support to the influence of peer interaction on the development of moral reasoning. When the results are compared, there was a greater change in the experimental group than in the control group. This suggests that the ability to interact and discuss moral situations with peers is influential in the development of moral reasoning. This would support Piaget's ideas. However, this study used a relatively small sample and therefore there are questions about generalisation. Also not all children benefited from peer interaction, but mainly those who were using lower levels of moral reasoning when the study began. This may suggest that peer interaction encourages children to develop their moral reasoning, but that once they have reached the higher levels of reasoning for their age they cannot advance beyond this. Again this would support a stage model, suggesting that development occurs in stages and that children need to be cognitively ready to move to the next stage.

Another issue is that these moral debates were created by the experimenters and so were somewhat artificial in nature. This may have affected the results. Finally children in the control group were given hypothetical problems; there was no way of knowing whether their behaviour would have mirrored their decisions. There is often a difference between moral judgements and moral behaviour. This study has shown that peer interaction can encourage the development of moral reasoning.

Glossary

accommodation. Revising an existing schema to take account of new learning.

animism. The tendency to attribute feelings and intentions to inanimate objects.

assimilation. The process of putting a new experience into already existing mental structure (schemas).

attrition. The dropout rate of participants in a study.

autonomous morals. Morals which are self-determined.

clinical interview. An open interview where questions are asked – like a doctor's appointment.

cognitive development. The study of how children develop their mental activities and processes, and become more efficient and effective in their understanding of the world and in their mental processes.

cohort effect. A particular group of children experience a unique set of events and conditions, which make this group different from others not of the same age.

collective punishment. The whole group is punished because the person in authority does not know who was at fault.

compensation. An alteration to an aspect of shape of an object, which does not alter the properties of the object.

concrete. Refers to a child's ability to apply strategies and rules to things that are present but not in an abstract manner.

conservation. The realisation that quantity or amount does not change when nothing has been added or taken away from an object or collection of objects, despite changes in form or spatial arrangements.

controlled observation. Observation of children's behaviour where some aspect is controlled, e.g. the situation.

cross-sectional studies. This method allows researchers to compare different age groups of children with each other at the same point in time.

developmental psychology. A study of the psychological changes and developments that occur across the lifespan. The focus is often development in childhood and adolescence.

egocentrism. Viewing the world from your perspective and being unable to understand any other perspective.

elementary mental functions. Natural and unlearned behaviours.

equilibration. The process of seeking to achieve cognitive stability through assimilation and accommodation.

ethnocentric. A view or theory derived from or focused upon a specific culture.

expert other. A more experienced learner with more developed strategies and understanding.

Flynn effect. The gradual rise in IQ levels observed over time.

heteronomous morals. Morals that are controlled and fixed by others.

higher mental functions. Aspects of cognition, which need to be developed through learning.

hypothetical deductive reasoning. Reasoning that uses deductive logic.

life span development. A study of the psychological changes and developments that occur across the life span.

longitudinal studies. Studies which use one sample group and test them periodically to identify developmental changes.

moral absolutes. Rules that are sacred and fixed, and cannot be changed.

moral behaviour. How individuals behave in a moral situation.

moral judgement. The decision about what is right and what is wrong.

moral orientations. The basis on which you make moral decisions.

moral stories or **vignettes.** Stories in which children are asked to make a moral judgement about another child's action.

M-space. The working memory or mental space available to the child.

naturalistic observation. Children are studied in their natural environments, and often they are unaware that they are being studied.

nature. Inherited factors especially genes – includes events that occur as the child naturally matures, e.g. puberty.

nurture. Refers to the environment the child develops in – this includes the experiences that each child has throughout their development.

object permanence. The knowledge that objects are always in existence even if you can't see them.

operations. Strategies and rules used by the child for interpreting and investigating the child's world.

peer mentoring. The use of peers to act as mentors, to help and encourage the development of other children.

pro-social behaviour. Behaviour which is intended to help another individual.

realism. Children see rules as real things.

reciprocity. Punishments given are equal to the wrongness of the behaviour.

relativism. Rules can be changed by mutual consent.

reversibility. Physical actions and mental operations can be reversed.

scaffolding. Providing support and advice while a less experienced learner develops their own strategies.

schema. A cognitive representation of activities or things.

symbolic representations. Using objects to represent other objects – to be symbols for them.

systematic problem solving. Solving problems in a systematic and logical manner.

zone of proximal development or **ZPD.** The distance between the actual developmental level and the potential level of the child.

References

Alarcan, M., Knopik, V.S., & DeFries, J.C. (2000). Covariation of mathematics achievement & general cognitive ability in twins. *Journal of Social Psychology*, *38*(1), 63–77.

Baillargeon, R. & Devos, J. (1991). Object permanence in young infants: further evidence. *Child Development*, *62*, 1227–46.

Bartels, M., Rietvald, M.J.H., Van Baal, G.C.M., & Boomsma, D.I. (2002). Genetic influences on the development of intelligence. *Behavior Genetics*, *32*(4), 237–249.

Bee, H. (2000). *The developing child* 9th Edition. Boston: Allyn & Bacon.

Bee, H. & Boyd, D. (2002). *Lifespan development* 3rd Edition. Boston: Allyn & Bacon.

Bell, D., Rothwell Hughes, E., & Rogers, J. (1975). *Area, weight and volume: Monitoring and encouraging children's conceptual development*. London: Nelson.

Bennet, N. & Dunne, E. (1991). The nature and quality of talk in co-operative classroom groups. *Learning and Instruction*, *1*(2), 103–8.

Benton, D. (2001). Micro-nutrient supplementation and the intelligence of children. *Neuroscience and Biobehavioral Reviews*, *25*(4), 297–309.

Benton, D. & Cook, R. (1991). Vitamin and mineral supplements improve intelligence scores and concentration. *Personality and Individual Differences*, *12*(11), 1151–8.

Berkman, D.S., Lescano, A.G., Gilman, R.H., Lopez, S.L., & Black, M.M. (2002). Effects of stunting, diarrhoeal disease and parasitic infection during infancy on cognition in late childhood: a follow-up study. *Lancet, 359*, 564–571.

Bernstein, B. (1971). *Classes, codes and control* Vol 1. London: Routledge and Kegan Paul.

Bersoff, D.M. & Miller, J.G. (1993). Culture, context and the development of moral accountability judgments. *Developmental Psychology, 29*, 664–676.

Birch, A. (1997). *Developmental psychology* 2nd Edition. Harmondsworth, UK: Penguin.

Blasi (1980). In W.C. Crain (1985). *Theories of development.* Englewood Cliffs, NJ: Prentice-Hall.

Blaye, A., Light, P., Joiner, R. & Sheldon, S. (1991). Collaboration as a facilitator of planning and problem solving on a computer based task. *British Journal of Educational Psychology, 61*, 431–83.

Bouchard, T.J., Lykken, D.T., McGue, M., Segal, N.L. & Tellegan, A. (1990). Sources of human psychological differences. The Minnesota study of twins reared apart. *Science, 250*, 223–250.

Bouchard, T. J. & McGue, M. (1981). Familial studies of intelligence – a review. *Science, 22*, 72–93.

Bower, T.G.R. (1982). *Development in infancy* 2nd Edition. New York: WH Freeman.

Brewer, S. (2001). *A child's world.* London: Headline.

Brownell, C.A. (1990). Peer social skills in toddlers: Competencies and constraints illustrated by same-age and mixed-age interaction. *Child Development, 61*, 836–848.

Bryant, P.E. & Trabasso, T. (1971). Transitive inferences and memory in young children. *Nature, 232*, 456–8.

Buck-Morss, S. (1975). Socio-economic bias in Piaget's theory and its implications for cross-cultural studies. *Human Development, 18*, 35–49.

Caldwell, B.M. & Bradley, R.M. (1978). *Home observation for measurement of the environment.* Little Rock: University of Arkansas.

Caplan, M.Z. & Hay, D.F. (1989). Preschoolers' response to peer distress and beliefs about bystander intervention. *Journal of Child Psychology, 30*, 231–42.

Capron, C. & Duyme, M. (1989). In H. Bee & D. Boyd (2002). *Lifespan development* 3rd Edition. Boston: Allyn & Bacon.

Cardwell, M., Clark, L., & Meldrum, C. (2000). *Psychology for A level*. London: HarperCollins.

Carey, S. (1985) *Conceptual change in childhood*. Cambridge, MA: MIT Press.

Case, R. (1985). *Intellectual development birth to adulthood*. New York: Academic Press.

Chandler, M. J., Greenspan, S., & Barenboum, C. (1973). Judgements of intentionality in response to videotaped and verbally presented moral dilemmas: the medium is the message. *Child Development*, *44*, 315–320.

Chi, M.T.H. (1978). *Knowledge, structures and memory development*. In R.S. Siegler (Ed) *Children's thinking: what develops?* Hillsdale, NJ: Lawrence Erlbaum Associates Inc.

Choudhary, R., Sharma, A., Agarwal, K.S., Kumar, A., Sreenivas, V., & Puliyel, J.M. (2002). Research Report. Building for the future; influence of housing on intelligence quotients of children in an urban slum. *Health Policy and Planning*, *17*(4), 420–424.

Colby, A. & Kohlberg, L. (1987). *The measurement of moral judgement*. Cambridge: Cambridge University Press.

Colby, A., Kohlberg, L., Gibbs, J. & Lieberman, M. (1983). A longitudinal study of moral development. *Monographs of the Society for Research in Child Development*, *48*(1–2), 200.

Cole, M., Gay, J., Glick, J.A. & Sharp, D.W. (1971). *The cultural context of learning and thinking*. New York: Basic Books.

Coles (1962). In Hummel (1998). *Cognitive development*. http://chiron.valdosta.edu/whuitt/col/cogsys/piaget.html

Craig, A.P. & Beishuizen, J.J. (2002). Psychological testing in a multicultural society: universal or particular competencies. *Journal of Pacific History*, *13*(2).

Crain, W.C. (1985). *Theories of development*. Englewood Cliffs, NJ: Prentice-Hall.

Crandell, L.E. & Hobson, L.P. (1999). Individual differences in young children's IQ. A social-developmental perspective. *Journal of Child Psychology and Psychiatry*, *40*(3), 455–464.

Crawford, P.D. (2001). Educating for moral ability: reflections on moral development based on Vygotsky's theory of concept formation. *Journal of Moral Education*, *30*(2), 113–129.

Daley, T.C., Whaley, S.E., Sigman, M.D., Espinosa, M.P. & Neumann, C. (2003). IQ on the rise: The Flynn Effect in rural Kenyan children. *Psychological Science*, *14*(3), 215–219.

Danner, F.W. & Day, M.C. (1977). Eliciting formal operations. *Child Development*, *48*, 1600–1606.

de Geus, E.J.C., Wright, M.J., Martin, N.G. & Boomsma, D.I. (2001). Editorial: Genetics of brain function and cognition. *Behaviour Genetics*, *31*(6), 489–495.

Donaldson, M. (1978). *Children's minds*. London: Fontana.

Edwards, C. (1980). In W.C. Crain (1985). *Theories of development*. Englewood Cliffs, NJ: Prentice-Hall, pp. 118–136.

Eisenberg, N. & Fabes, R.A. (1991). Prosocial behavior and empathy: a multimethod, developmental perspective. In M. Clark (Ed) *Review of Personality and Social Psychology*, 12: 34–61. Newbury Park, CA: Sage.

Eisenberg, N., Miller, P.A., Shell, R., McNalley, S., & Shea, C. (1991). Prosocial development in adolescence: A longitudinal study. *Developmental Psychology*, *27*(5), 849–857.

Eisenberg, N., Shell, R., Paternak, J., Lennon, R., Beller, R. & Mathy, R.M. (1987). Prosocial development in adolesence: a longitudinal study. *Developmental Psychology*, *27*, 811–57.

Eisenberg-Berg, N. & Hand, M. (1979). The relationship of pre-schoolers' reasoning about prosocial moral conflicts to prosocial behaviour. *Child Development*, *50*, 356–63.

Emler, N. (1987). Socio-moral development from the perspective of social representations. *Journal for the Theory of Social Behaviour*, *17*, 371–388.

Eysink, T.H.S., Dijkstra, S. & Kuper, J. (2001). Cognitive processes in solving variants of computer-based problems used in logic teaching. *Computers in Human Behavior*, *17*(1) 1–19.

Ferguson, T.J. & Rule, B.G. (1982). Influence of inferential set, outcome intent and outcome severity on children's moral judgements. *Developmental Psychology*, *18*, 843–851.

Flanagan, C. (1997). *A level psychology*. London: Letts Educational.

Flanagan, C. & Eysenck, M.W. (2000). *Psychology for AS level*. Hove, UK: Psychology Press.

Frank, J.Z. (1966). In C. Flanagan *A level psychology* (1997). London: Letts Educational.

Fruend (1990). In C. Flanagan *A level psychology* (1997). London: Letts Educational.

Garlick, D. (2002). Understanding the nature of the general factor of intelligence, the role of individual differences in neural plasticity as an explanatory mechanism. *Psychological Review, 109*(1), 116–136.

Gibbs, J.S. & Schnell, M. (1985). In A. Birch (1997) *Developmental psychology* 2nd Edition. Harmondsworth, UK: Penguin.

Gilligan, C. (1982). *In a different voice: Psychological theory and women's development.* Cambridge, MA: Harvard University Press.

Gilligan, C. & Attanucci, J. (1988). Two moral orientations: gender differences and similarities. *Merrill Palmer Quarterly, 34,* 223–37.

Gick, E. (2003). Cognitive theory and moral behaviour: the contribution of F.A. Hayek to business ethics. *Journal of Business Ethics, 45*(1–2), 149–165.

Gredler, M. (1992). *Learning and instruction into practice.* New York: Macmillian Publishing Company.

Gzesh, S. M. & Surber, C.F. (1985). Visual perspective-taking skills in children. *Child Development, 56,* 1204–1213.

Harland, T. (2003). Vygotsky's zone of proximal development and problem-based learning: linking a theoretical concept with practice through action research. *Teaching in Higher Education, 8*(2), 263–272.

Hart, B. & Risley, T. (1995). *Meaningful difference in the everyday experiences of young American children.* Baltimore, MD: Paul Brooks.

Hasse, C. (2001). Institutional creativity: the relational zone of proximal development. *Culture and Psychology, 7*(2), 199–221.

Heath, S.B. (1989). Oral and literate traditions among Black Americans living in poverty. *American Psychologist, 44,* 367–73.

Hedge, A. & Yousif, Y.H. (1992). The effect of urban size, cost and urgency on helpfulness: a cross cultural comparison between the United Kingdom and the Sudan. *Journal of Cross-cultural Psychology, 23,* 107–15.

Helwig, C.C., Tisak, M.S. & Turiel, E. (1990). Children's social reasoning in context: a reply to Gabennesch. *Child Development, 61,* 2068–2078.

Hippisley, J. (2001). Vygotsky's zone of proximal development. http://www.interactived.com/vygotsky.com

Hoffung, S. (1997). *Child and adolescent development*. Boston: Houghton Mifflin Company.

Holstein, C.B. (1976). Irreversible, step wise sequence in the development of moral judgement: a longitudinal study of males and females. *Child Development, 47*, 51–66.

Holton, D., Ahmed, A., Williams, H. & Hill, C. (2001). On the importance of mathematical play. *International Journal of Mathematical Education in Science and Technology, 32*(3), 401–415.

Hooper, H. & Walker, M. (2002). Makaton peer tutoring evaluation: 10 years on. *British Journal of Learning Disabilities, 30*(1), 38–42.

Horn, J.M. (1983). The Texas Adoption Project: adopted children and their intellectual resemblance to biological and adoptive parents. *Child Development, 544*, 266–275.

Houdee, O. & Guichart, E. (2001). Negative priming effect after inhibition of number/length interference in a Piaget-like task. *Developmental Science, 4*(1).

Hummel, J. (1998). *Cognitive development*. http:/chiron.valdosta.edu/whitt/col/cogsys/piaget.html

Humphries, M.L., Parker, B.L. & Jagers, R.J. (2000). Predictors of moral reasoning among African American children: a preliminary study. *Journal of Black Psychology, 26*(1), 51–64.

Inhelder, B. & Piaget, J. (1958). *The growth of logical thinking from childhood to adolescence*. London: Routledge & Kegan Paul.

Kail, R. (1990). *Development of memory in children*. New York: Oxford University Press.

Kamii, C. & DeVries, R. (1978). *Physical knowledge in preschool education: implications of Piaget's theory*. Englewood Cliffs, NJ: Prentice Hall.

Kamin, L.J. (1977). *The science and politics of IQ*. Harmondsworth, UK: Penguin.

Kaufman, A.S. (1999). Genetics of childhood disorder II: genetics and intelligence. *Journal of the American Academy of Child and Adolescent Psychiatry, 38*(4), 487–88.

Kline, P. (1991). *Intelligence: The psychometric view*. London: Routledge.

Kohlberg, L. (1963). The development of children's orientation towards a moral order. Sequence in the development of moral thought. *Vita Humana*, *6*, 11–33.

Kohlberg, L. (1969). Stage and sequence the cognitive development approach to socialization. In D.A. Goslin (Ed) *Handbook of socialization theory and research*. Chicago, IL: McNally.

Kohlberg, L. (1976). Moral stages and moralism. In T. Linkons (Ed) *Moral development and behavior*. New York: Holt, Rinehart and Winston.

Kohlberg, L. (1984). *Essays on moral development*, Vol 1, *The philosophy of moral development*. New York: Harper & Row.

Kohlberg, L. & Kramer, R. (1969). Continuities and discontinuities in childhood and adult moral development. *Human Development*, *12*, 93–120.

Kruger, A.C. (1992). The effect of peer and adult–child transitive discussions on moral reasoning. *Merrill Palmer Quarterly*, *38*, 191–211.

Labov, W. (1970). The logic of non-standard English. In J.E. Alatis (Ed) *20th Annual Round Table*. Washington: University Press.

Landry, S.H. (1996). In H. Bee & D. Boyd (2002). *Lifespan development* 3rd Edition. Boston: Allyn & Bacon.

Lange, G. (1973). The development of conceptual and rote recall skills among school age children. *Journal of Experimental Child Psychology*, *15*, 394–406.

Laupa, M. (1991). Children's reasoning about the three authority attrubutes adult status, knowledge and social position. *Developmental Psychology*, *27*(2), 321–329.

Laupa, M. & Turiel, E. (1986). Children's conceptions of adult and peer authority. *Child Development*, *57*, 405–412.

LeFrancois, G.R. (1994). *Psychology for teaching*. Belmont, CA: Wadsworth Publishing Company.

Lenaerts, J., Wieme, W. & Zele, E.V. (2003). Peer instruction: a case study for an introductory magnetism course. *European Journal of Physics*, *24*(1), 7–14.

Light, P., Buckingham, N. & Robbins, A.H. (1979). The conservation task as an interactional setting. *British Journal of Educational Psychology*, *49*, 304–310.

Linaza, J. (1984). Piaget's marbles: the study of children's games and their knowledge of rules. *Oxford Review of Education*, *10*, 271–4.

Loehlin, J.C. & Horn, J.M. (2000). Stoolmiller on restriction of range in adoption studies: a comment. *Behavior Genetics, 30*(3), 245–247.

Loehlin, J.C., Horn, J.M. & Willerman, L. (1989). Modeling IQ change: evidence from the Texas Adoption Project. *Child Development, 60*, 993–1004.

Lowery, S. (1995). *The effect of birth order on intelligence.* http://www.mwsc.edu/~p...y302/fall95/lowery.htm

Luckin, R., Connolly, D., Plowman, L. & Airey, S. (2003). Children's interactions with interactive toy technology. *Journal of Computer Assisted Learning, 19*(2), 165–176.

Luedecke, S., Zirkel, A. & Beck, K. (1998). Vocational training and moral judgement – a critical review. *International Journal of Educational Research, 27*(7), 605–617.

Luna, A.R. (1992). *Ape, primitive man and child: essays in the history of behavior.* Baltimore, MD: Deutsch Press.

Luo, Y., Baillargeon, R., Brueckner, L. & Munakata, M. (2003). Reasoning about a hidden object after a delay: evidence for robust representations in 5-month old infants. *Cognition, 88*(3), 23–32.

Lyons, N.P. (1983). Two perspectives: on self, relationships and morality. *Harvard Educational Review, 53*, 125–57.

Mastropieri, M.A., Scruggs, T.E., Spencer, V. & Fontana, J. (2003). Promoting success in high school world history: peer tutoring versus guided learning. *Disabilities Research & Practice, 18*(1), 52–65.

McDonald, L. & Stuart-Hamilton, I. (2003). Egocentrism in older adults – Piaget's three mountains task revisited. *Educational Gerontology, 29*(5), 417–425.

McGarrigle, J. & Donaldson, M. (1974). Conservation accidents. *Cognition, 3*, 341–50.

McGilly, K. & Sieglar, R.S. (1989). How children choose among serial recall strategies. *Child Development, 55*, 172–82.

McNayton, S. & Leyland, J. (1990). Maternal regulations of children's problem solving behaviour and its impact on children's performance. *Child Development, 61*, 113–126.

Meltzoff, A.N. & Moore, M.K. (1998). Object representation, identity, and the paradox of early permanence: steps toward a new framework. *Infant Behaviour and Development, 21*(2), 201–235.

Midlarsky, E. & Hannah, M.E. (1985). Competence, reticence and helping by children and adolescents. *Developmental Psychology*, *21*, 534–541.

Miller, J.G. et al. (1990). Perceptions of social responsibilities in India and the United States: moral imperative on personal decisions. *Journal of Personality and Social Psychology*, *58*, 33–47.

Miller, J.G. & Bersoff, D.M. (1992). Culture and moral judgment: How are conflicts between justice and interpersonal responsibilities resolved. *Journal of Personality and Social Psychology*, *26*, 541–554.

Miller, P., Mulvey, C. & Martin, N. (2001). Genetic environmental contributions to educational attainment in Australia. *Economics of Education Review*, *20*(3).

Mones, A.G., & Haswell, E.L. (1998). Morality as a verb: the process of moral development within the "family culture". *Journal of Social Distress and the Homeless*, *7*(2), 91–105.

Moore, C. & Frye, D. (1986). The effect of the experimenter's intention on the child's understanding of conservation. *Cognition*, *22*, 283–98.

Narvaes, D. (2001). Moral text comprehension: implications for education and research. *Journal of Moral Education*, *30*(1), 43–54.

Nelson, K. (1980). Constraints on word learning. *Cognitive Development*, *3*, 221–246.

Newman, H.M. (1928). Studies of Human Twins II. Asymmetry reversal of mirror imaging in identical twins. *Biological Bulletin*, *55*, 298–315.

Pederson, N.L., Plomin, R. & McClearn, G.E. (1994). Is there G beyond 'g'? (is there genetic influence on specific cognitive abilities independent of genetic influence on general cognitive ability?) *Intelligence*, *18*, 133–143.

Pederson, N.L., Plomin, R., Nesselroade, J.R. & McClearn, G.E. (1992). A quantitative genetic analysis of cognitive abilities during the second half of the lifespan. *Psychological Science*, *3*(6), 346–53.

Peterson, C.C. & Siegal, M. (2002). Mindreading and moral awareness in popular and rejected preschoolers. *British Journal of Developmental Psychology*, *20*(2), 205–224.

Peterson, L. (1983). Role of donor competence, donor age and peer presence on helping in an emergency. *Developmental Psychology*, *19*, 873–880.

Piaget, J. (1932). *The moral judgement of the child*. Harmondsworth, UK: Penguin.

Piaget, J. (1936/1952). *The origin of intelligence in the child*. London: Routledge & Kegan Paul.

Piaget, J. (1954). *The construction of reality in the child*. New York: Basic Books.

Piaget, J. (1972). *The psychology of the child*. New York: Basic Books.

Piaget, J. & Inhelder, B. (1956). *The child's conception of space*. London: Routledge & Kegan Paul.

Pianta, R.C. & Egeland, B. (1994). Relation between depressive symptoms and stressful life events in a sample of disadvantaged mothers. *Journal of Consulting and Clinical Psychology*. In H. Bee & D. Boyd (2002). *Lifespan development* 3rd Edition. Boston: Allyn & Bacon.

Plomin, R. (1997). Identifying genes for cognitive abilities and disabilities. In R.J. Sternberg & E.L. Grigorenko (Eds) *Intelligence: heredity and environment*. New York: Cambridge University Press.

Plomin, R. (1988). *Nature and nurture during infancy and early childhood*. New York: Academic Press.

Plomin, R. & DeFries, J.C. (1979). Multivariate behavioral genetic analysis of twin data on scholastic abilities. *Behavior Genetics*, *9*, 505–517.

Plomin, R. & Petrill, S.A. (1997). Genetics and intelligence: what's new? *Intelligence*, *24*(1), 53–77.

Pramling, N. & Samuelsson I.P. (2001). "It is floating 'cause there is a hole'": a young child's experience of natural science. *Early years: Journal of International Research and Development*, *21*, 139–149.

Prior, W. (2001). Read in your head: a Vygotskian analysis of the transition from oral to silent reading. *Reading Psychology*, *22*(1), 1–15.

Pulaski, M.A.S. (1980). *Understanding Piaget*. New York: Harper & Row Publishers.

Radke-Yarrow, M. & Zahn Waxler, C. (1984). Root motives and patterns in children's prosocial behavior. In R. Vasta, M. Haith & S.A. Miller (Eds) *Child psychology: the modern science* (1999) 3rd Edition. New York: Wiley.

Ramey, C.T. (1993). In H. Bee & D. Boyd (2002). *Lifespan development* 3rd Edition. Boston: Allyn & Bacon.

Ramey, C.T. & Campbell, F.A. (1987). In H. Bee & D. Boyd (2002). *Lifespan development* 3rd Edition. Boston: Allyn & Bacon.

Rest, J.R. (1983a). Morality. In P. Mussen, J.H. Flavell & E.M. Markman (Eds) *Handbook of child psychology*, Vol 3. New York: Wiley.

Rest, J.R. (1983b). In W.C. Crain (1985). *Theories of development*. Englewood Cliffs, NJ: Prentice-Hall, pp. 118–136.

Richardson, K. (1999). *Understanding intelligence*. Buckingham, UK: Open University Press.

Richardson, K. (2002). What IQ tests test. *Theory and Psychology*, *12*(3), 283–314.

Rodgers, J.L., Cleveland, H.H., Van den Oord, E. & Rowe, D.C. (2001). Resolving the debate over birth order, family size and intelligence. *American Psychologist, 55*, 599–612.

Rose, S.A. & Blank, M. (1974). The potency of context in children's cognition. An illustration through conservation. *Child Development, 45*, 499–502.

Rosenthal, R. & Jacobson, L. (1968). *Pygmalion in the classroom: teacher expectation and pupils' intellectual development*. New York: Rinehart & Winston.

Sameroff, A.J. et al. (1987). Familial role and child competence. *Child Development, 54*, 1254–68.

Sameroff, A.J., Seifer, R., Baldwin, A.L. & Baldwin, C.A. (1993). Stability of intelligence from pre-school to adolescence: the influence of social and family risk factors. *Child Development, 64*, 80–97.

Samuel, S. & Bryant, P. (1984). In C. Flanagan *A level psychology* (1997). London: Letts Educational.

Scarr, S. & Weinberg, R.A. (1977). IQ test performance of black children adopted by white families. *American Psychologist, 31*, 726–39.

Scarr, S. & Weinberg, R.A. (1983). The Minnesota Adoption Studies, genetic differences and malleability. *Child Development, 54*, 260–7.

Schewdar, R.A. (1990). In defense of moral realism: Reply to Gabennesch. *Child Development, 61*, 2060–2067.

Schiff, M. et al. (1978). In C. Flanagan *A level psychology* (1997). London: Letts Educational.

Segal, N., Weisfeld, G.E. & Weisfeld, C.C. (Eds) (1997). Uniting psychology and biology. *Interactive perspectives on human development.* New York: American Psychological Association.

Shields, J. (1962). *Monozygotic twins brought up apart and brought up together.* London: Oxford University Press.

Siegal, M. (1982). *Fairness in children: a social-cognitive approach in the study of moral development.* London: Academic Press.

Siegler, R.S. (1988). *Children's thinking* 3rd Edition. Englewood Cliffs, NJ: Prentice Hall.

Sigman, M. et al. (1988). In H. Bee & D. Boyd (2002). *Lifespan development* 3rd Edition. Boston: Allyn & Bacon.

Simpson, E.L. (1974). In W.C. Crain (1985). *Theories of development.* Englewood Cliffs, NJ: Prentice-Hall, pp. 118–136.

Sims, R., Dobbs, G. & Hand, T. (2002). Enhancing quality in online learning: scaffolding planning and design through proactive evaluation. *Distance Education, 32*(2), 135–148.

Sinclair-de-Zwart, H. (1969). Developmental linguistics. In D. Elkind & J.H. Favell (Eds) *Studies in cognitive development.* Oxford: Oxford University Press.

Slavin, R. E. (1994). *Educational psychology. Theory and practice* 4th Edition. Boston: Allyn & Bacon.

Smetana, J.G. (1981). Preschool children's conceptions of moral and social rules. *Child Development, 52,* 1333–6.

Smetana, J.G. (1999). The role of parents in moral development: a social domain analysis. *Journal of Moral Education, 28*(3), 311–321.

Smith, P.K., Cowie, H. & Blades, M. (1998). *Understanding children's development* 3rd Edition. Oxford: Blackwell.

Smith, R. (2001). *Going beyond Piaget.* http://www.camalott.com/rssmith/piaget.html

Snarey, J.R. (1985). Cross-cultural universality of social–moral development: a critical review of Kohlbergian research. *Psychological Bulletin, 97,* 202–32.

Snarey, J.R., Reimer, J. & Kohlberg, L. (1985). Development of social–moral reasoning among kibbutz adolescents: a longitudinal cross-cultural study. *Developmental Psychology, 21,* 3–17.

Sternberg, R.J. & Wagner, R.K. (Eds) (1986). Practical intelligence: nature and origins of competence in the everyday world. Cambridge: Cambridge University Press.

Stone, S. (1995). *The primary multiage classroom: changing schools for children*. Unpublished manuscript.

Stoolmiller, M. (1998). Correcting estimates of shared environment variance for range restriction in adoption studies using a truncated multivariate normal model. *Behavior Genetics, 28*(6), 429–441.

Sutherland, P. (1982). In P. Sutherland (1999). The application of Piagetian and neo-Piagetian ideas to further and higher education. *International Journal of Lifelong Education, 18*(4), 286–294.

Sutherland, P. (1999). The application of Piagetian and neo-Piagetian ideas to further and higher education. *International Journal of Lifelong Education, 18*(4), 286–294.

Thornton, D. & Reid, R.I. (1982). Moral reasoning and type of criminal offence. *British Journal of Social Psychology, 21,* 231–238.

Tibbetts, S.G. (1999). Differences between women and men regarding decisions to commit test cheating. *Research in Higher Education, 40*(3), 323–342.

Turiel, E. (1983). The development of social knowledge: morality and convention. Cambridge: Cambridge University Press.

Vygotsky, L. (1987). The development of scientific concepts in childhood. In R.W. Rieber & A.S. Carton (Eds) *The collected works of LS Vygotsky* Vol 1. New York: Plenum Press.

Wahlsten, J. (1990). Gene map of mental retardation. *Journal of Mental Deficiency Research, 34,* 11–27.

Walker, L. (1984). Sex differences in the development of moral reasoning: a critical review. *Child Development, 55,* 677–91.

Walker, L. & Mann, L. (1987). Unemployment, relative deprivation and social protest. *Personality and Social Psychology Bulletin, 13,* 275–287.

Walker, L.J. (1999). The family context of moral development. *Journal of Moral Education, 28*(3), 261–264.

Walker, L.J., deVries, B. & Trevethan, S.D. (1987). Moral stages and moral orientations in real-life and hypothetical dilemmas. *Child Development, 58,* 842–58.

Weinreich-Haste, H. (1982). Piaget on morality: a critical perspective. In S. Modgil & C. Modgil (Eds) *Jean Piaget: consensus and controversy*. London: Holt, Rinehart & Winston.

Whiting, B. & Whiting, J.W.M. (1975). *Children of six cultures*. Cambridge, MA: Harvard University Press.

Woolfolk, A.E. & McCune-Nicolich, L. (1984). *Educational*

psychology for teachers 2nd Edition Englewood Cliffs, NJ: Prentice-Hall, Inc.

Youniss, J. & Volpe, J. (1978). In W.C. Crain (1985). *Theories of development*. Englewood Cliffs, NJ: Prentice-Hall.

Zahn Waxler, C., Radke-Yarrow, M., Wagner, E. & Chapman, M. (1992). Development of concern for others. *Developmental Psychology*, *28*, 126–136.

Zajonc, R.B. (2001). The family dynamics of intellectual development. *American Psychologist*, *56*, 490–496.

Zajonc, R.B. & Markus, G.B. (1975). Birth order and intellectual development. *Psychological Review*, *82*, 74–88.

Zigler, E.F., Abelson, W.D. & Seitz, V. (1973). Motivational factors in the performance of economically disadvantaged children on the Peabody Picture Vocabulary Test. *Child Development*, *44*, 294–303.

Index